MARK MULLE

THE BIG BOOK OF DRAWING FOR MINECRAFTERS

HOW TO DRAW MORE THAN 75 MINECRAFT MOBS AND ITEMS

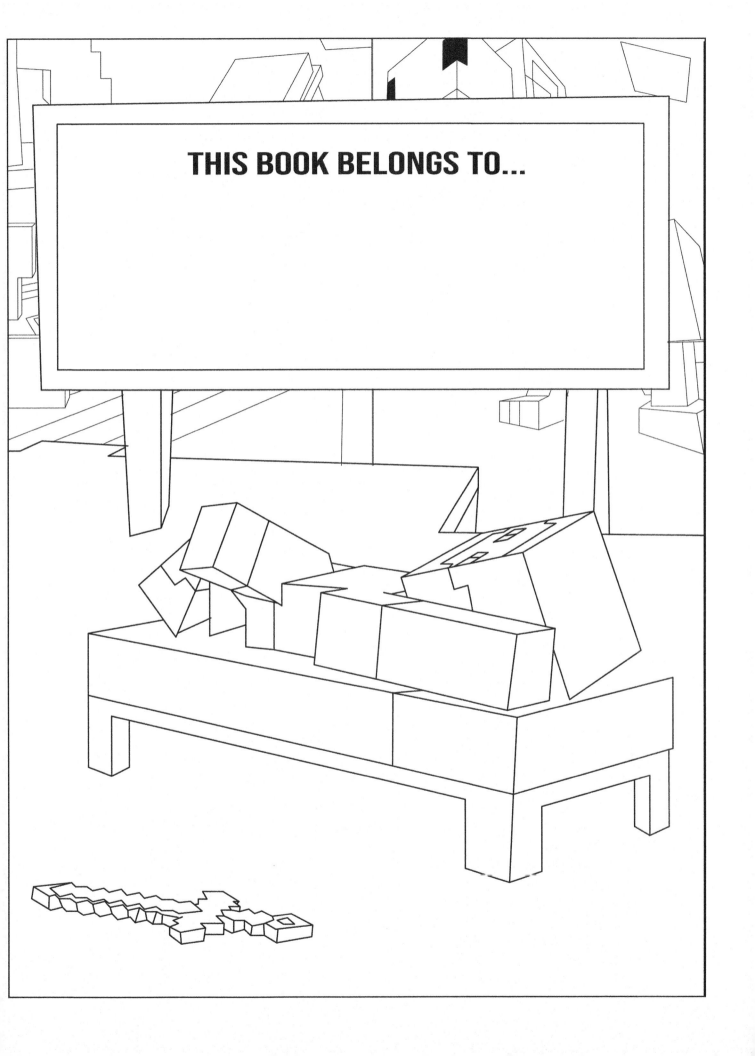

THIS BOOK BELONGS TO...

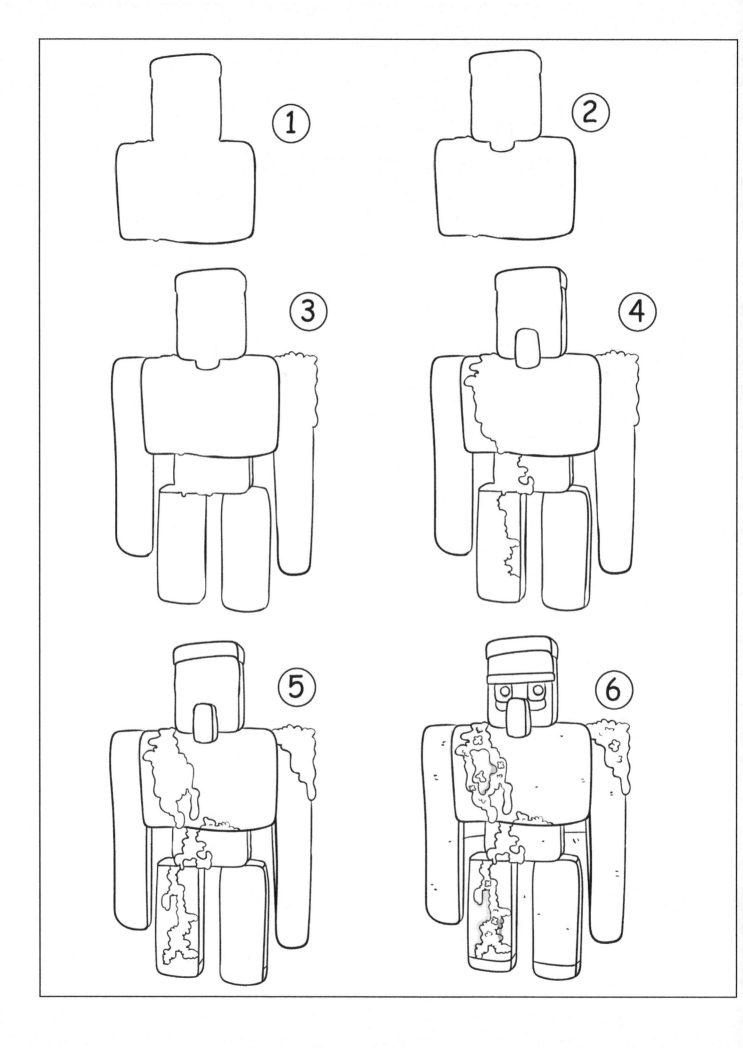

Now, it's your turn

STEVE

DIFFICULTY LEVEL

1 FIRST DRAW THE SHAPE OF STEVE'S HEAD AND TORSO.

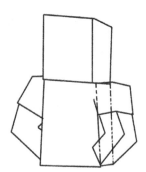

2 DRAW HIS HANDS. ERASE DOTTED LINES.

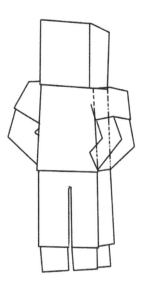

3 NEXT STEP IS EASY JUST FOLLOW OUR LEAD. DRAW HIS LEGS.

4 ALMOST DONE! NOW WHEN YOU HAVE THE SHAPE OF STEVE'S BODY USE THICKER LINES TO DRAW HIS FINAL SHAPE.

5 FEW MORE DETAILS AND OUR STEVE IS DONE! ADD HIM A FACE, SOME SHADING AND HE IS READY.

Now, it's your turn

MAGMA CUBE

DIFFICULTY LEVEL
♥ ♥ ♡ ♡ ♡

1 THIS IS SUPER EASY, SO LET'S BEGIN. FIRST, DRAW A FUNNY SHAPED SQUARE.

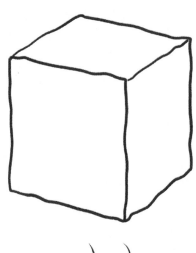

2 NOW FORM A CUBE BY ADDING THE SIDES OF THE SQUARE.

3 ALMOST DONE! DRAW IT A FACE AND SOME DETAILS TO MAKE YOUR MAGMA CUBE SUPER HOT!

Now, it's your turn

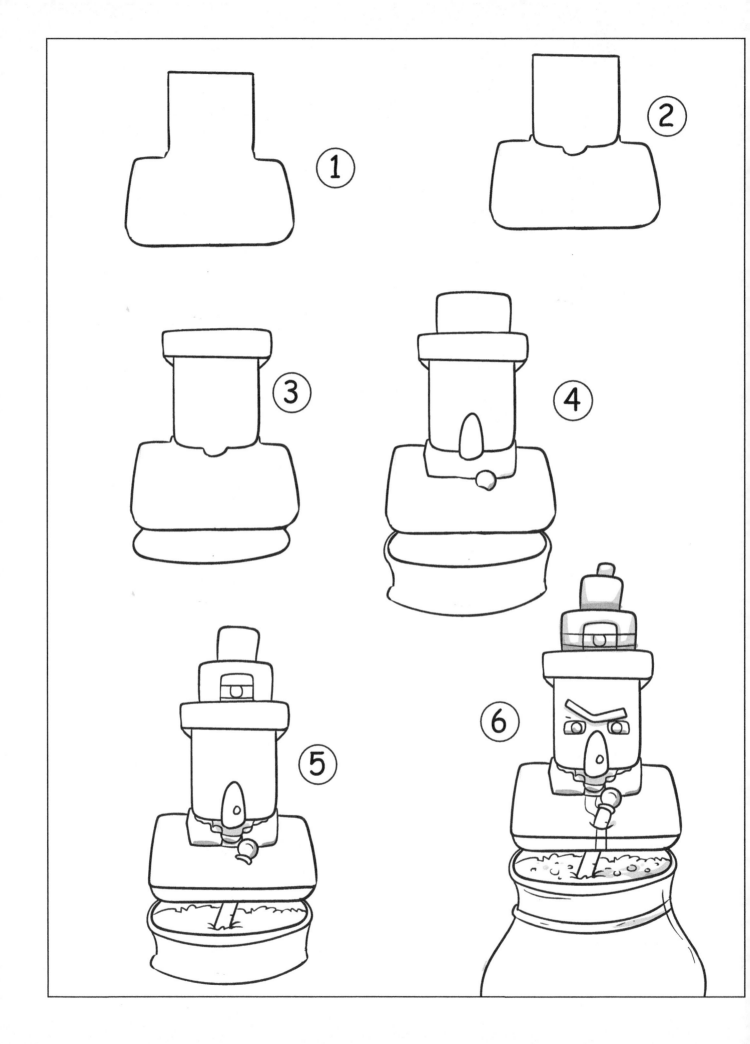

Now, it's your turn

CREEPER

DIFFICULTY LEVEL

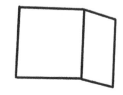

1 FIRST DRAW THE SHAPE OF A CREEPER'S HEAD.

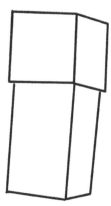

2 DRAW A RECTANGULAR CUBOID BELOW HIS HEAD TO CREATE HIS TORSO.

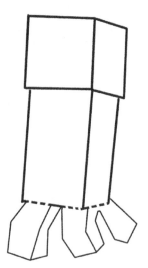

3 NEXT DRAW HIS LEGS.

4 ALMOST DONE! NOW WHEN YOU HAVE THE SHAPE OF THE CREEPER USE THICKER LINES TO DRAW HIS FINAL SHAPE.

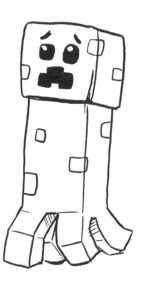

5 FEW MORE DETAILS AND OUR CREEPER IS DONE! ADD HIM A FACE, SOME SPOTS AND HE IS DONE.

Now, it's your turn

 **BED**

1 LET'S START WITH THIS SHAPE. IT IS A LARGE RECTANGULAR PRISM.

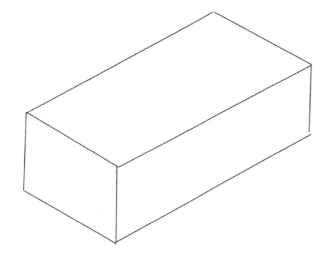

2 SHAPE YOR BED AND ITS LEGS BY FOLLOWING NEXT SIMPLE STEP. ERASE DOTTED LINE.

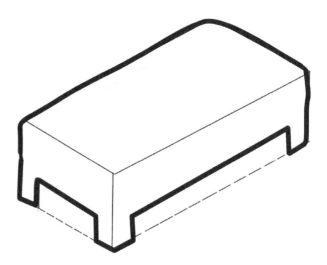

3 ALMOST DONE! NOW YOU CAN DRAW THE BLANKET AND SEPARATE THE PARTS OF THE BED.

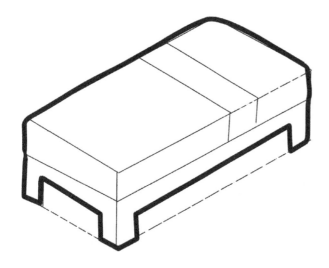

4 ALMOST DONE! USE THINNER LINES TO DRAW PILLOW AND SMALL DETAILS, AND YOU HAVE A COZY BED!

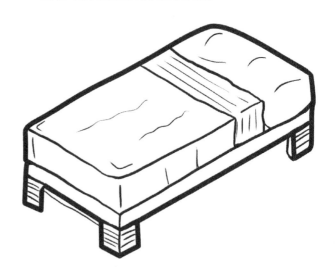

Now, it's your turn

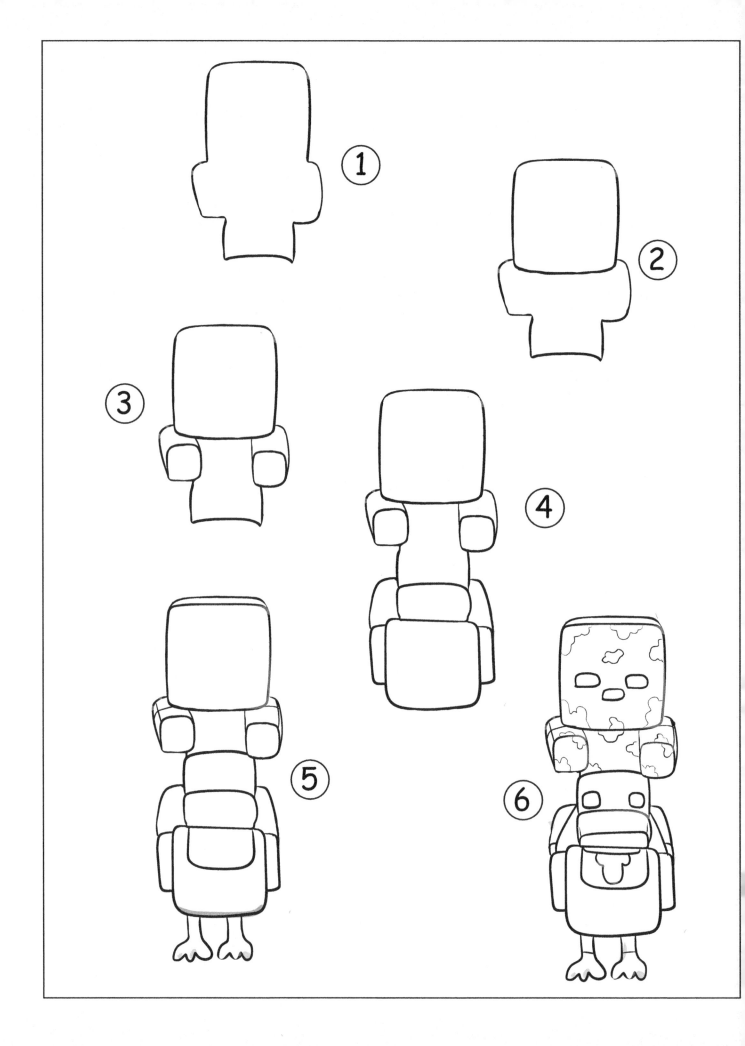

Now, it's your turn

BAT

DIFFICULTY LEVEL

1 START WITH DRAWING THE SHAPE OF THE BAT'S HEAD AND TORSO.

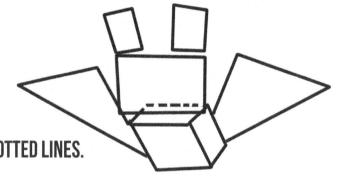

2 THEN DRAW HIS WINGS AND EARS. ERASE DOTTED LINES.

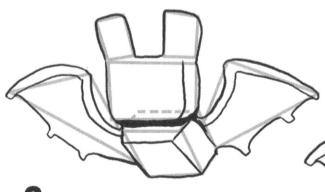

3 NEXT STEP IS EASY. JUST FOLLOW OUR GUIDELINES FOR HIS BODY.

4 ALMOST DONE! NOW WHEN YOU HAVE THE SHAPE OF THE BAT USE THICKER LINES TO DRAW HIS FINAL SHAPE. DRAW THE BAT'S FACE AND SOME LINES FOR SHADINGS.

Now, it's your turn

ENDER-CHEST

1 TO FORM THE SHAPE OF AN ENDER-CHEST, LET'S START WITH ONE BIG, BORING CUBE!

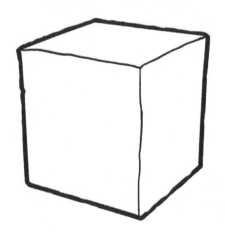

2 DRAW TWO LINES TO SEPARATE ITS TOP FROM THE BOTTOM.

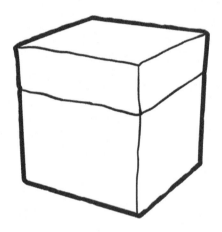

3 NOW, LET'S DRAW IT A LOCK. IT LOOKS LIKE A SMALL RECTANGULAR CUBOID, LYING AT THE MIDDLE LINE WHICH SEPARATES THE TOP FROM THE BOTTOM.

4 ALMOST DONE! NOW YOU CAN FINISH YOUR IMAGE BY ADDING DETAILS ON YOUR ENDER-CHEST.

Now, it's your turn

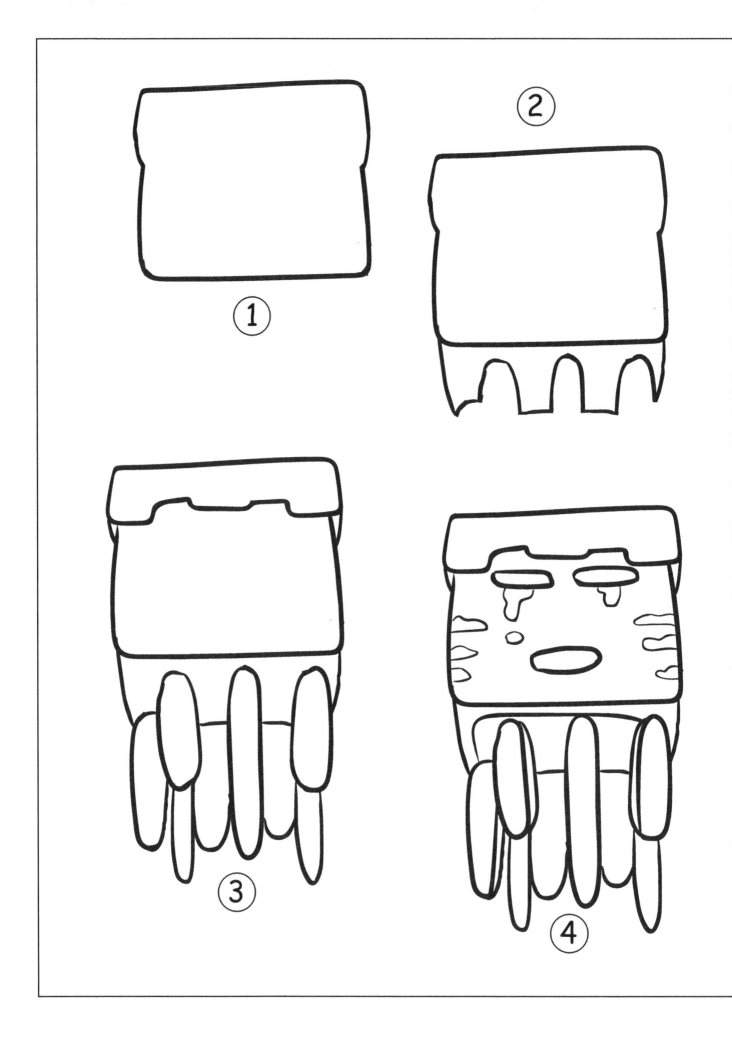

Now, it's your turn

CHICKEN

DIFFICULTY LEVEL

1 FIRST DRAW THE SHAPE OF THE CHICKEN'S HEAD AND TORSO.

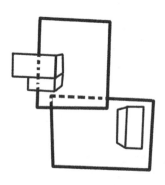

2 NOW DRAW ITS BEAK AND WING ERASE DOTTED LINES.

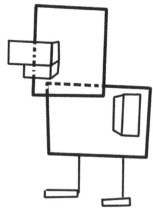

3 NEXT STEP IS EASY. JUST FOLLOW OUR LEAD AND DRAW ITS LEGS.

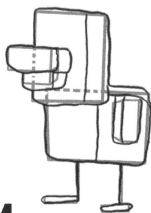

4 ALMOST DONE! NOW WHEN YOU HAVE THE SHAPE OF THE CHICKEN USE THICKER LINES TO DRAW HIS FINAL SHAPE.

5 FEW MORE DETAILS AND OUR CHICKEN IS DONE! ADD ITS FACE, SOME SHADING AND IT IS DONE.

Now, it's your turn

Now, it's your turn

Now, it's your turn

RABBIT

DIFFICULTY LEVEL

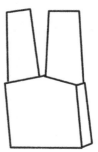

1 DRAW THE SHAPE OF THE RABBIT'S HEAD AND EARS.

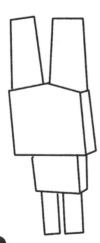

2 DRAW HIS TORSO AND HIS FRONT LEGS.

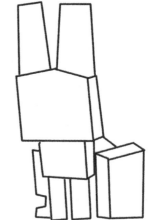

3 NEXT STEP IS EASY, DRAW HIS BACK LEGS.

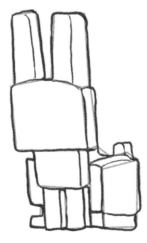

4 ALMOST DONE! NOW YOU HAVE THE SHAPE OF THE RABBIT.

5 DRAW THE RABBIT'S FACE. ADD A FEW MORE DETAILS AND SHADING AND OUR RABBIT IS DONE.

Now, it's your turn

 **BOOK**

1 LET'S DRAW A BOOK. START BY DRAWING A PARALLELOGRAM AS LINE GUIDE. IN STEP 1A, TRACE THE OUTLINE OF THE BOOK

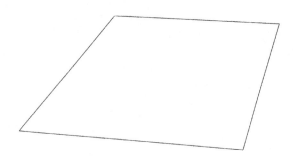

2 DRAW A THIN CUBOID AT THE BOTTOM AND AT THE EDGE OF THE BOOK AS LINE GUIDES. IN STEP 2A, DRAW A MIDDLE VERTICAL LINE ON THE BOOK TO MAKE ITS PAGES AND ADD CURVE LINES AT THE BOTTOM.

3 REMOVE THE LINE GUIDES OF THE BOOK. TO MAKE YOUR DRAWING LOOK MORE REALISTIC, WRITE AND DRAW ANYTHING ON THE PAGES OF THE BOOK.

Now, it's your turn

Now, it's your turn

DIFFICULTY LEVEL

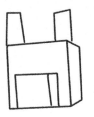

1 START WITH DRAWING THE COW'S HEAD AND EARS.

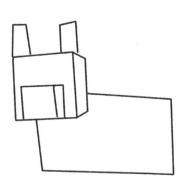

2 NOW DRAW COW'S TORSO

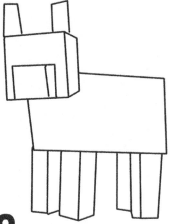

3 NEXT STEP IS TO DRAW ITS LEGS

4 ALMOST DONE! TRACE WITH THICKER LINES THE FINAL SHAPE OF THE COW

5 DRAW ITS FACE. ADD A FEW MORE DETAILS LIKE SPOTS, TAIL AND SOME SHADING.

Now, it's your turn

JUKEBOX

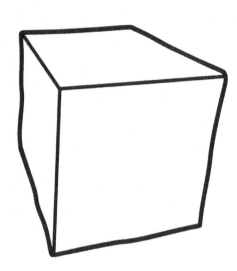

1 START WITH A CUBE, JUST LIKE THIS ONE:

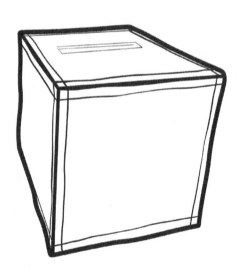

2 DRAW THICKER LINES ON ITS EDGES AND HORIZONTAL LINES ON TOP OF THE CUBE.

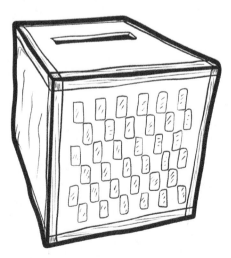

3 ALMOST DONE! FINISH OFF THIS DRAWING BY ADDING DETAILS ON THE BODY OF THE JUKEBOX

Now, it's your turn

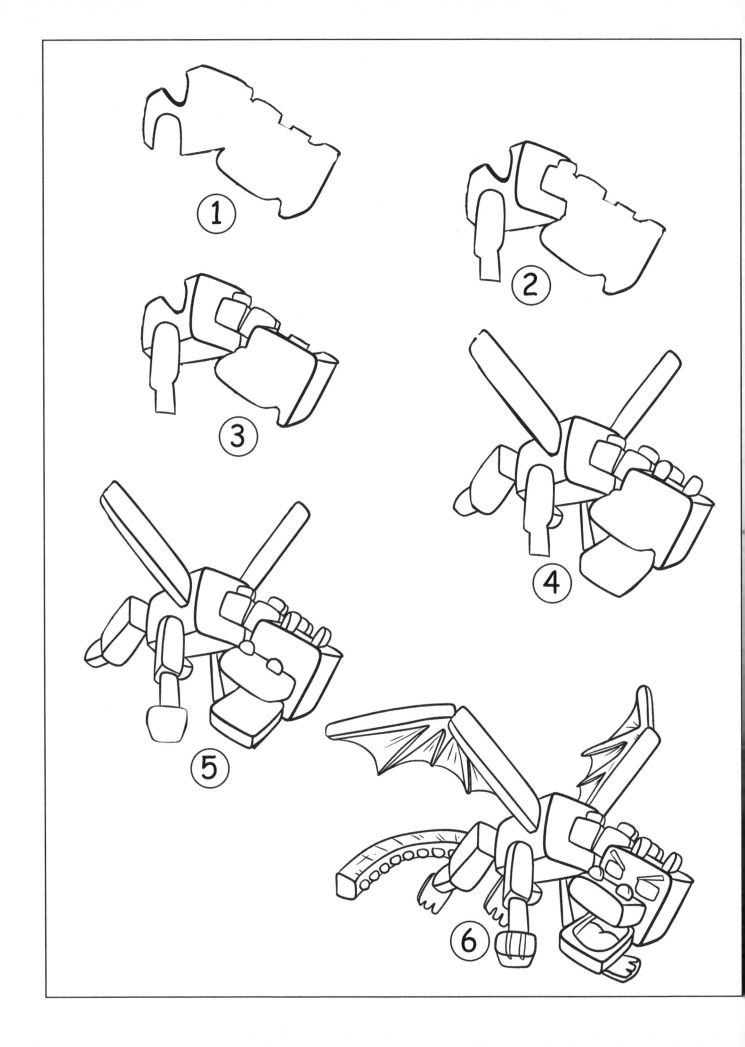

Now, it's your turn

TULIP

DIFFICULTY LEVEL

1 FIRST DRAW A STEM.

2 NEXT DRAW THE SHAPE OF THE FLOWER.

3 ADD SOME LEAVES.

4 NOW ADD MORE LEAVES TO OUR PLANT'S STEM.

5 ADD FEW MORE DETAILS TO BRING OUR TULIP TO LIFE AND ITS DONE.

Now, it's your turn

SHEEP

DIFFICULTY LEVEL

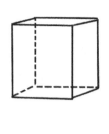 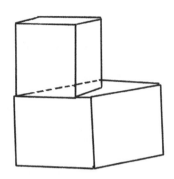

1 FIRST DRAW THE SHAPE OF THE SHEEP'S HEAD.

2 ADD LEGS AND SHEEP'S TAIL

3 ALMOST DONE, NOW YOU HAVE THE SHAPE OF THE SHEEP.

4 ADD FACE FEATURES, EARS AND SOME SHADING AND YOU ARE DONE.

Now, it's your turn

Now, it's your turn

MOOSHROOM

DIFFICULTY LEVEL

1 FIRST DRAW CUBE FOR MOOSHROOM'S HEAD AND ADD ITS EARS AND SNOUT.

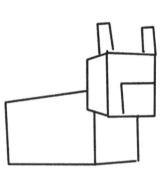

2 NEXT DRAW ITS TORSO

3 ADD ITS LEGS

4 ALMOST DONE, DRAW ITS TAIL

5 ADD FACE FEATURES, SPOTS, MUSHROOMS, AND SOME SHADING AND YOU ARE DONE.

Now, it's your turn

DIFFICULTY LEVEL

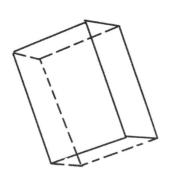

1 FIRST DRAW THIS SHAPE FOR SQUID'S HEAD.

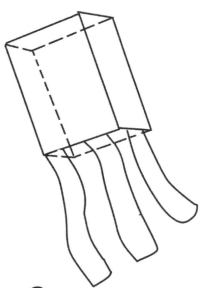

2 NOW ADD A FEW TENTACLES

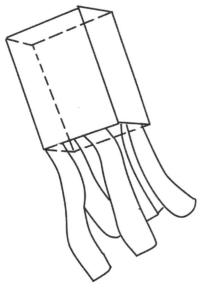

3 ADD MORE TENTACLES AND ERASE DOTTED LINES

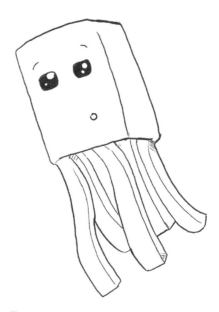

4 ALMOST DONE, NOW YOU HAVE THE SHAPE OF THE SQUID, ADD ITS FACE FEATURES AND SOME SHADING AND THAT IS IT.

Now, it's your turn

SPIDER

DIFFICULTY LEVEL

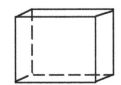
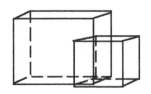

1 START WITH A CUBOID. DRAW A SMALLER CUBE BESIDE IT AS SHOWN IN THE IMAGE.

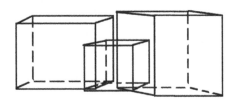

2 NEXT DRAW ANOTHER BIGGER CUBE ON THE OTHER SIDE OF THE SMALLER CUBE TO COMPLETE THE SPIDER'S BODY.

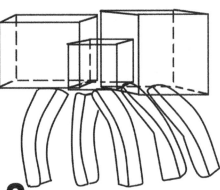

3 ADD LEGS TO OUR SPIDER'S BODY AND ERASE DOTTED LINES.

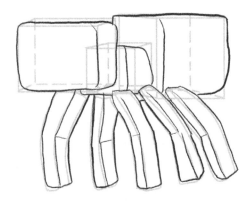

4 ALMOST DONE, NOW YOU HAVE THE SHAPE OF THE SPIDER.

5 ADD FACE FEATURES AND SOME SHADING AND YOU ARE DONE.

Now, it's your turn

ANVIL

1 OKAY, THESE STEPS ARE EASY SO LET'S BEGIN. FIRST, DRAW A THIN RECTANGLE. DRAW ANOTHER RECTANGLE BELOW THE FIRST ONE BUT THIS RECTANGLE IS THICKER AS SHOWN IN IMAGE 1A. FEEL FREE TO REMOVE THE DOTTED LINES.

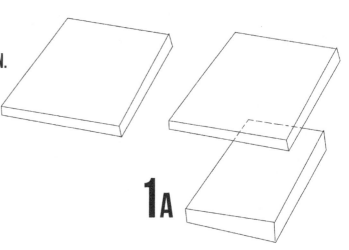

1A

2 DRAW TWO LINES CONNECTING YOUR TWO RECTANGLES TO FORM THE FINAL SHAPE OF YOUR ANVIL. ADD THE HORN OF THE ANVIL AS SHOWN IN 2A.

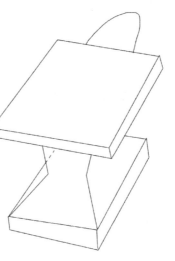

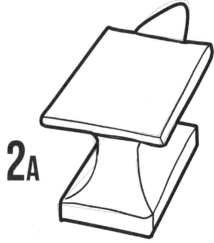

2A

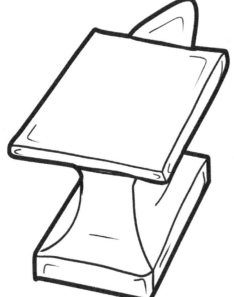

3 ALMOST DONE! ADD SOME DETAILS ON YOUR ANVIL TO MAKE IT LOOK REALISTIC.

Now, it's your turn

Now, it's your turn

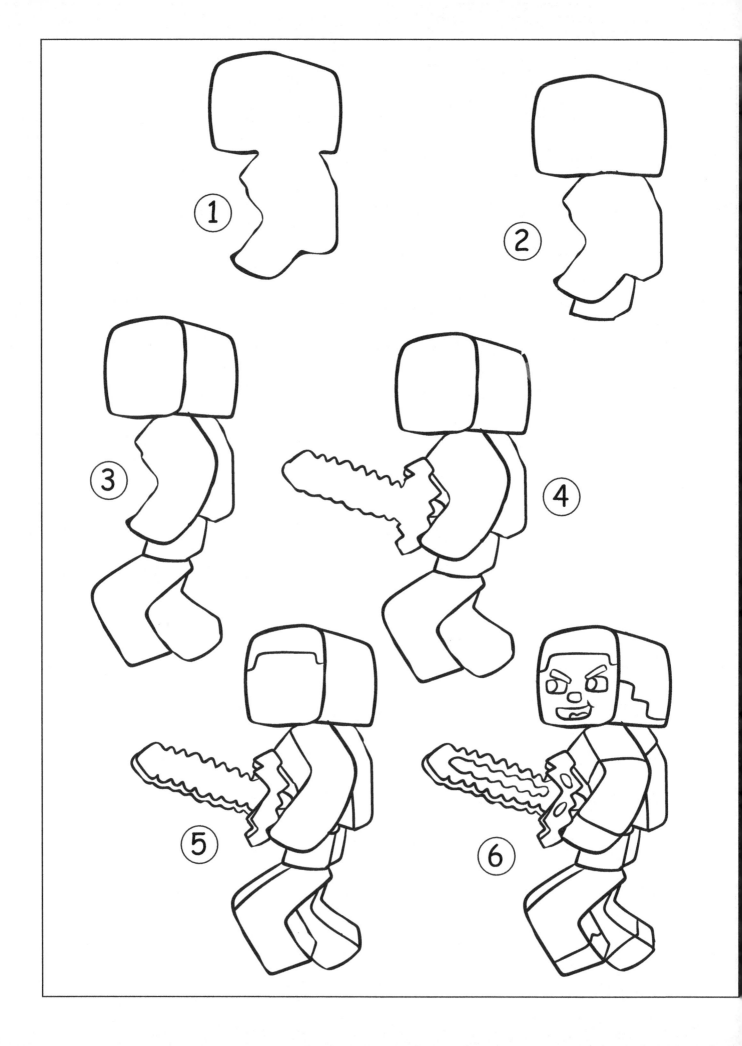

Now, it's your turn

DIFFICULTY LEVEL

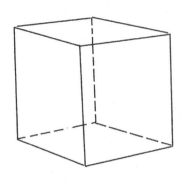

1 FIRST DRAW A CUBE

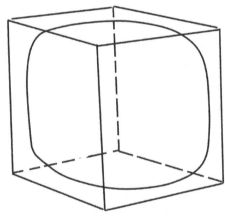

2 NEXT DRAW THIS SHAPE WHITIN THE CUBE.

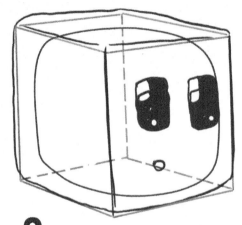

3 ADD HIS FACE AND ERASE DOTTED LINES

4 ALMOST DONE, NOW JUST ADD SOME FINAL DETAILS.

Now, it's your turn

ENDERMAN

DIFFICULTY LEVEL

1 FIRST DRAW A CUBE FOR THE ENDERMAN'S HEAD AND ADD HIS TORSO.

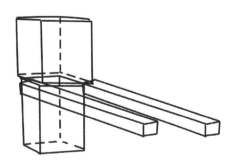

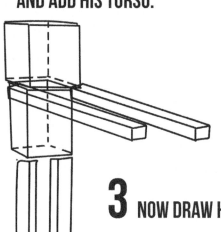

3 NOW DRAW HIS LEGS.

2 NEXT DRAW HIS HANDS LIKE THIS.

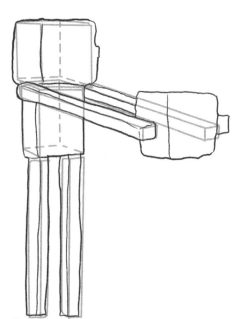

4 ALMOST DONE, DRAW A BLOCK BETWEEN THE HANDS OF THE ENDERMAN

5 ADD FACE FEATURES, SOME DETAILS, SOME SHADING AND YOU ARE DONE.

Now, it's your turn

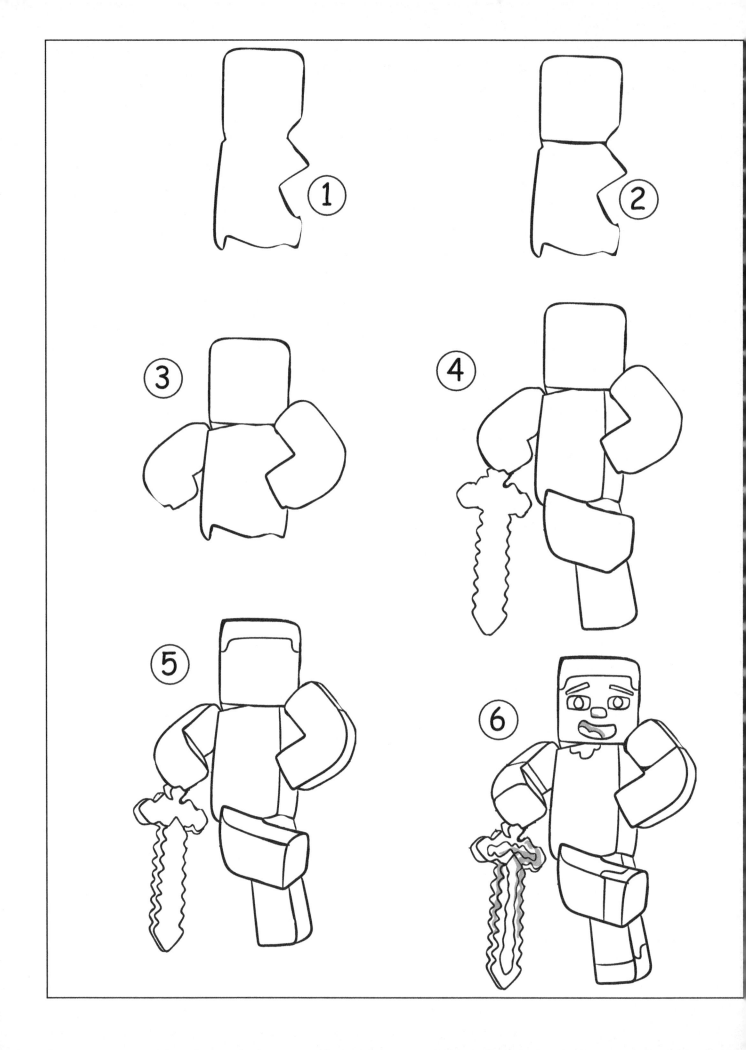

Now, it's your turn

ENCHANTMENT TABLE

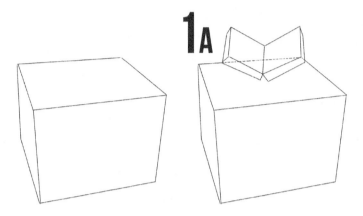

1 LET'S START OFF BY DRAWING A BOX. THEN ADD TWO CUBOIDS ON TOP OF THE BOX NEAR THE UPPER EDGE AS SHOWN IN IMAGE 1A.

2 AT THIS STAGE, LET'S DRAW SOMETHING THAT LOOKS ROUGHLY LIKE AN OPEN BOOK. THEN DRAW THE BOOK COVER AND DRAW ONE PAGE OF THE BOOK AS SHOWN IN IMAGE 2A. SHADE THE OUTER LINES OF THE BOOK AND THE ENCHANTMENT TABLE.

3 ADD DETAILS ON YOUR ENCHANTMENT TABLE AND PUT WRITINGS OR DRAWINGS ON YOUR BOOK TO FINISH OFF THE IMAGE.

Now, it's your turn

Now, it's your turn

SNOW GOLEM

DIFFICULTY LEVEL

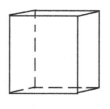

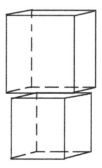

1 FIRST DRAW CUBE FOR HIS HEAD AND ANOTHER ONE FOR HIS TORSO.

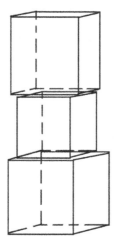

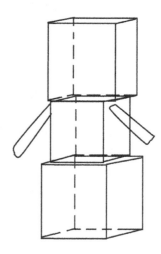

2 NEXT DRAW ANOTHER CUBE TO GET HIS FULL BODY SHAPE .

3 ADD HIS ARMS AND ERASE DOTTED LINES.

4 ALMOST DONE, NOW DRAW HIS FACE.

5 ADD MORE DETAILS AND SOME SHADING AND YOU ARE DONE.

Now, it's your turn

CAKE

DIFFICULTY LEVEL

1 OK, THIS IS EASY. SO LETS BEGIN. DRAW THIS SHAPE.

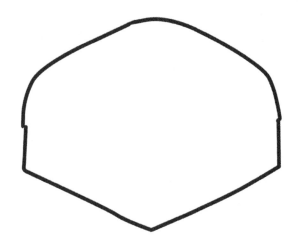

2 NOW TO MAKE IT LOOK LIKE A CAKE, DRAW ITS SIDES AND ADD CREAM ON TOP.

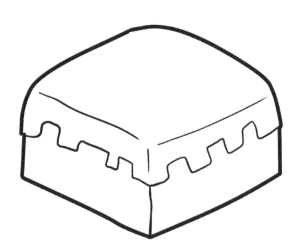

3 ALMOST DONE! ALL YOU HAVE TO DO IS DRAW A CANDLE AND ADD DETAILS AND SHADINGS ON YOUR CAKE.

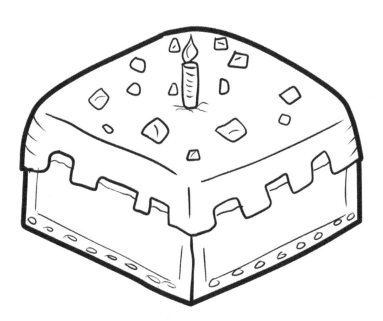

Now, it's your turn

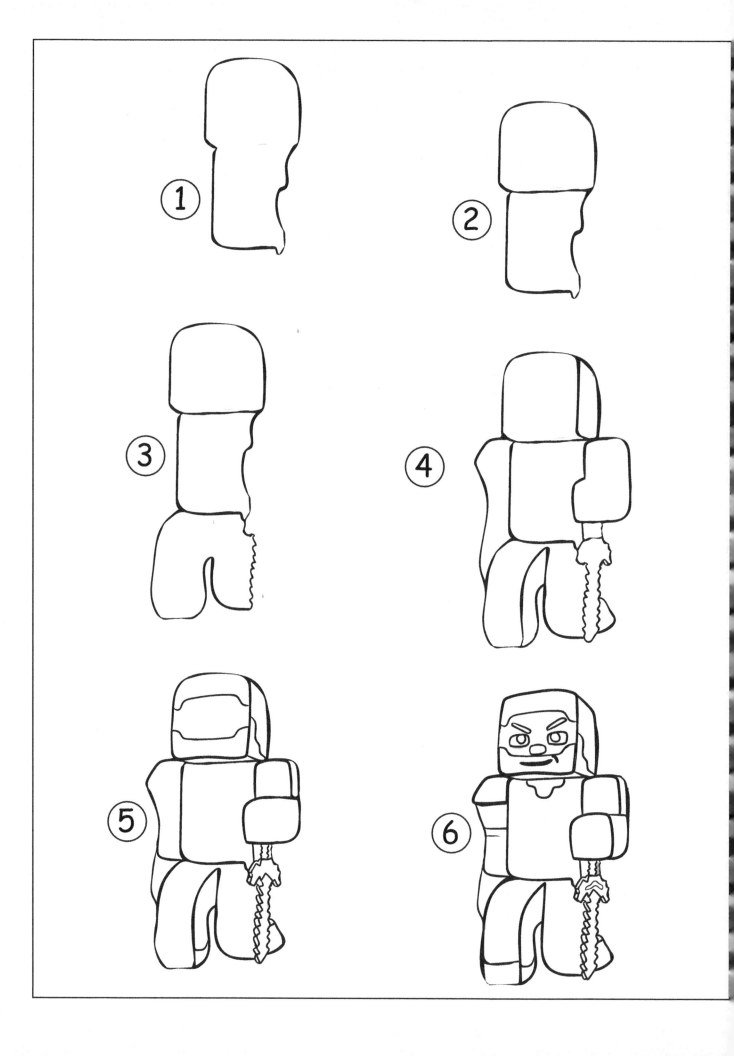

Now, it's your turn

Now, it's your turn

BOW AND ARROW

DIFFICULTY LEVEL

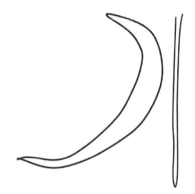

1 FIRST DRAW MAIN SHAPE OF BOW AND LINE FOR ARROW.

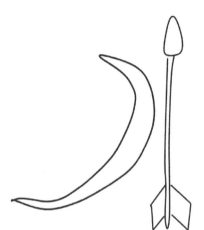

2 NEXT DRAW THESE SHAPES FOR ARROW.

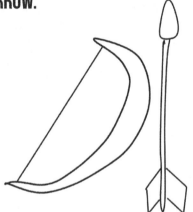

3 ADD A LINE FOR BOW'S STRING.

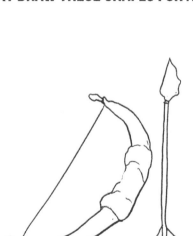

4 ALMOST DONE, NOW DRAW SOME DETAILS.

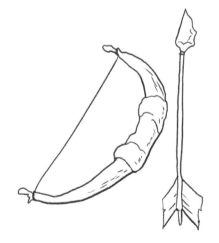

5 ADD FEW DETAILS AND SOME SHADING AND YOU ARE DONE.

Now, it's your turn

ALEX

1 LET'S START OFF BY DRAWING ALEX'S HEAD. DRAW A CUBE, THEN ADD THICKER LINES TO THE CUBE AND FINALLY ADD ALEX'S HAIR BANGS AND EAR.

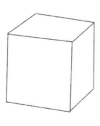  

2 TO MAKE ALEX'S TORSO, DRAW A CUBOID BELOW ALEX'S HEAD. DRAW ALEX'S ARMS AT THE SIDES OF HER TORSO AS YOU CAN SEE IN STEP 2A.

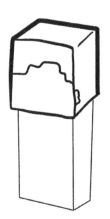

2A

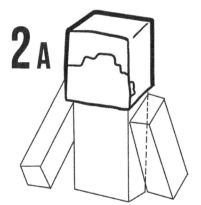

3 AT THIS STAGE, DRAW TWO RECTANGULAR CUBOIDS BELOW ALEX'S TORSO FOR HER LEGS.

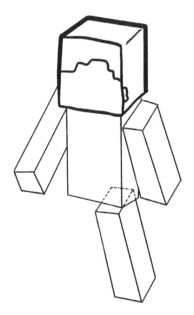 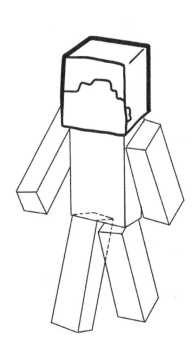

Now, it's your turn

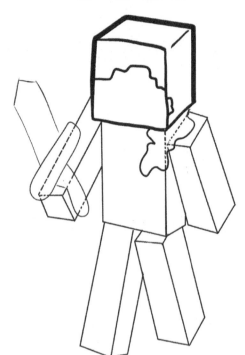

4 NOW THAT HER BODY IS COMPLETE, LET'S DRAW A SWORD ON HER RIGHT HAND.

5 USE THICKER LINES TO OUTLINE HER BODY AND ADD HER LONG HAIR TOO

6 TO FINISH DRAWING ALEX, ADD HER EYES, NOSE AND MOUTH. ADD SOME SHADING AND OTHER DETAILS ON HER CLOTHES AND HAIR.

Now, it's your turn

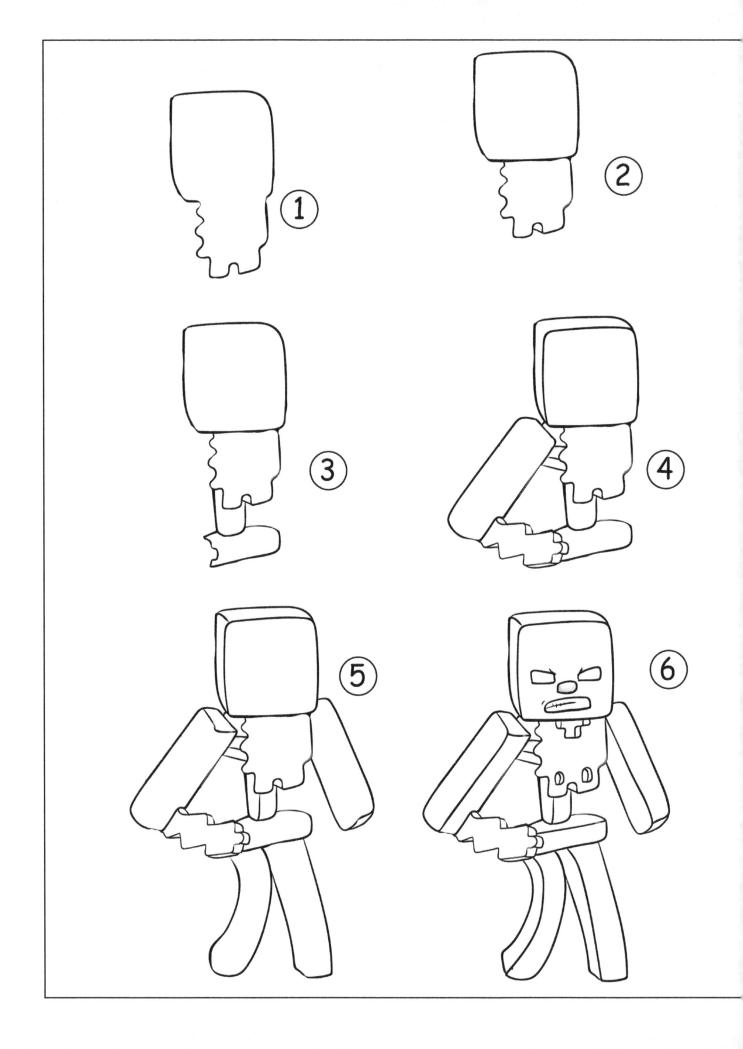

Now, it's your turn

DIFFICULTY LEVEL

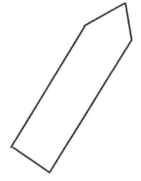

1 FIRST DRAW THIS SHAPE FOR BLADE

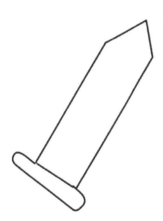

2 NEXT DRAW THIS SHAPE

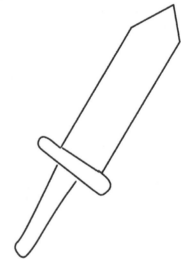

3 NEXT ADD THIS SHAPE FOR HANDLE

4 ALMOST DONE, NOW YOU HAVE THE MAIN SHAPE OF THE SWORD.

5 ADD SOME DETAILS AND SHADING LINES AND YOU ARE DONE.

Now, it's your turn

AXE

DIFFICULTY LEVEL

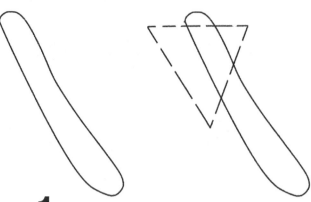

1 FIRST DRAW THIS SHAPE FOR AXE'S HANDLE AND DRAW A TRIANGLE.

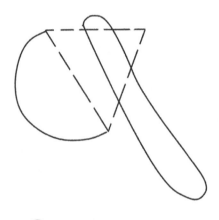

2 NEXT DRAW THIS SHAPE TO HAVE THE BLADE PART OF THE AXE.

3 FOLLOW THE SHAPE ABOVE AND REMOVE THE EXCESS LINES.

4 ALMOST DONE, NOW YOU HAVE MAIN SHAPE OF AXE

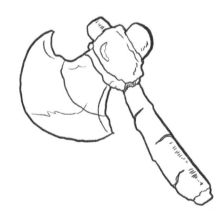

5 ADD SOME DETAILS, LINES AND SOME SHADING AND YOU ARE DONE.

Now, it's your turn

Now, it's your turn

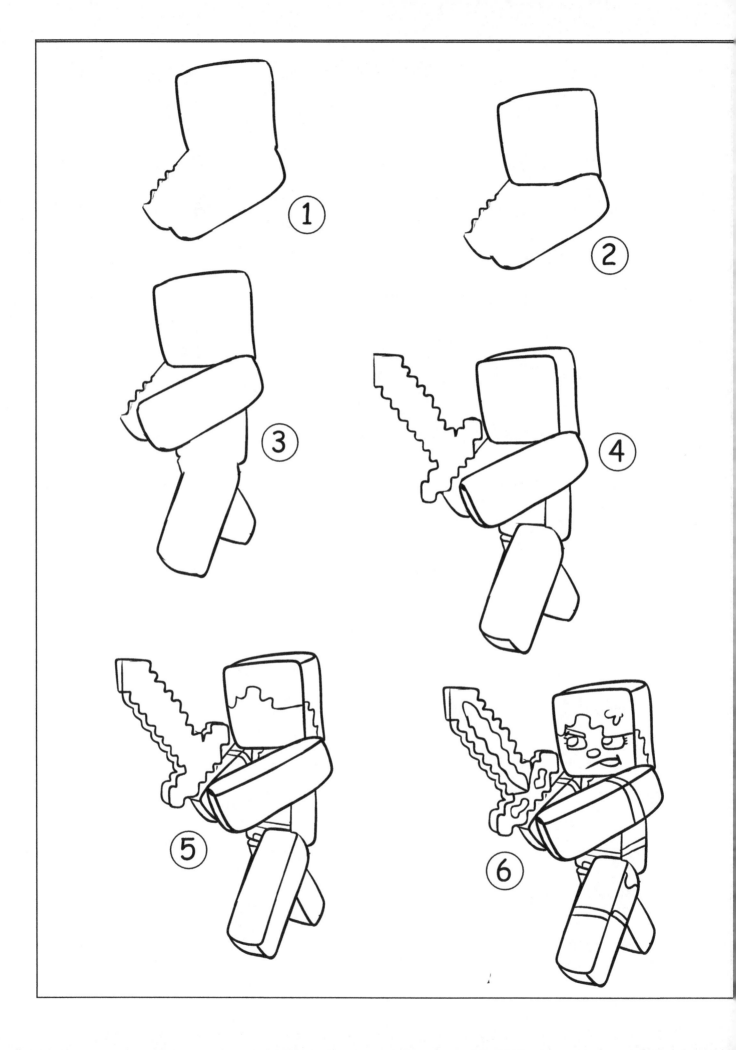

Now, it's your turn

GUARDIAN

DIFFICULTY LEVEL

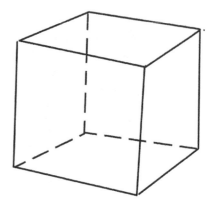

1 FIRST DRAW CUBE FOR GUARDIAN'S HEAD.

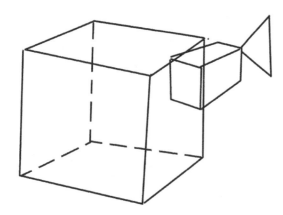

2 NEXT DRAW THESE SHAPES FOR HIS TAIL AND FIN

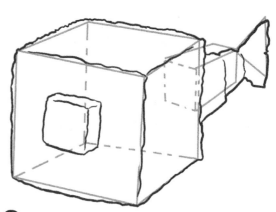

3 ADD A SMALL CUBE FOR HIS EYE

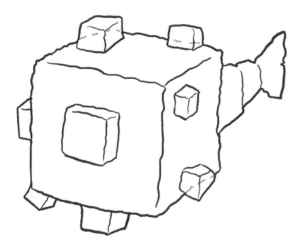

4 ALMOST DONE, NOW DRAW FEW MORE CUBE SHAPES FOR BUMPS ON HIS BODY

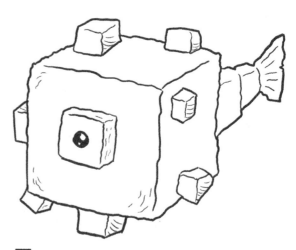

5 ADD DETAILS FOR HIS EYE, SOME LINES, SOME SHADING AND THAT IS IT

Now, it's your turn

WITHER

DIFFICULTY LEVEL

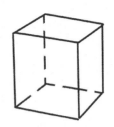

1 FIRST DRAW CUBE FOR WITHER'S HEAD.

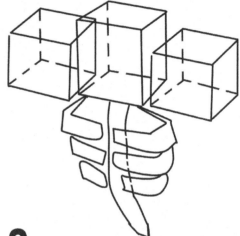

2 ADD TWO MORE CUBES

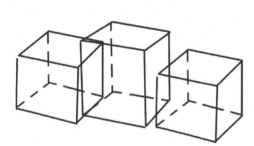

3 NEXT DRAW LINES FOR HIS BODY
TO GET THIS SHAPE LIKE THIS

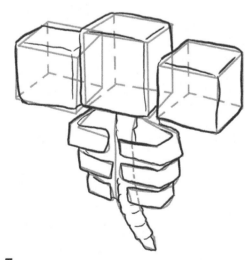

4 ALMOST DONE! NOW YOU HAVE THE MAIN
SHAPE OF THE WITHER. ERASE DOTTED LINES.

5 ADD FACE FEATURES, SOME DETAILS
SOME SHADING AND OUR WITHER IS DONE.

Now, it's your turn

Now, it's your turn

IRON GOLEM

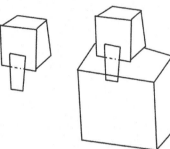

DIFFICULTY LEVEL

1 FIRST DRAW THIS SHAPE FOR GOLEM'S HEAD AND DRAW HIS TORSO.

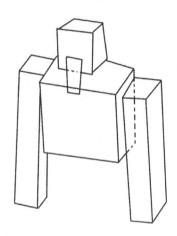

2 ADD HIS ARMS AS SHOWN IN THE IMAGE.

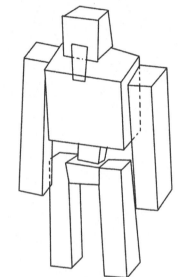

3 THEN ADD LOWER PART OF HIS BODY AND LEGS.

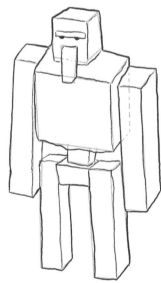

4 ALMOST DONE, DRAW HIS FACE AND ERASE DOTTED LINES AND NOW YOU HAVE THE SHAPE OF THE GOLEM.

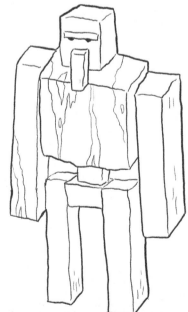

5 ADD SOME LINES FOR TEXTURE AND SOME SHADING AND THAT IS IT..

Now, it's your turn

OCELOT

DIFFICULTY LEVEL

♥ ♥ ♥ ♥ ♡

1 FIRST, DRAW A CUBE FOR THE OCELOT'S HEAD.

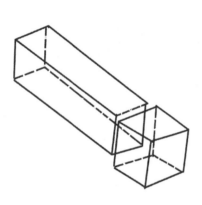

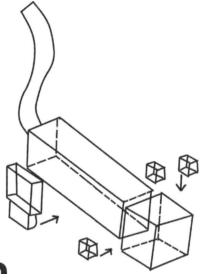

2 NEXT DRAW THIS SHAPE FOR ITS TORSO

3 ADD LEGS, EARS AND OCELOT'S TAIL.

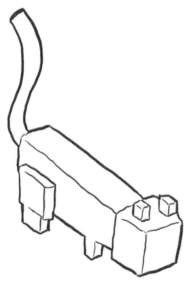

4 ALMOST DONE, ERASE DOTTED LINES AND NOW WE HAVE MAIN SHAPE OF OCELOT

5 ADD FACE FEATURES, LINES AND SOME SHADING AND YOU ARE DONE.

Now, it's your turn

Now, it's your turn

LLAMA

DIFFICULTY LEVEL

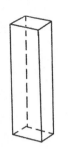 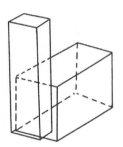

1 FIRST DRAW THE SHAPE OF THE LLAMA'S BODY.

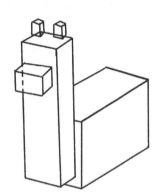

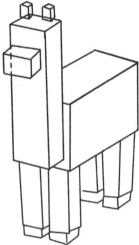

2 NEXT ERASE DOTTED LINES AND ADD EARS AND SNOUT

3 NOW ADD LLAMA'S LEGS.

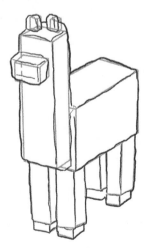

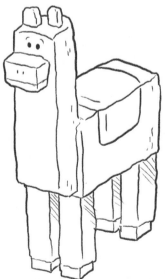

4 ALMOST DONE, NOW YOU HAVE THE SHAPE OF THE LLAMA.

5 ADD FACE FEATURES, ITS SADDLE AND SOME SHADING AND YOU ARE DONE.

Now, it's your turn

LILAC

DIFFICULTY LEVEL

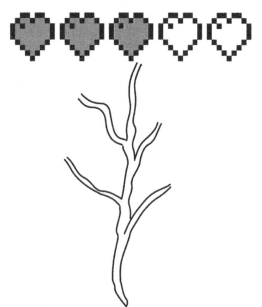

1 FIRST DRAW STEM OF LILAC.

2 ADD FLOWERS TO OUR PLANT.

3 ALMOST DONE, NOW ADD SOME LEAVES.

4 ADD FEW MORE DETAILS TO BRING OUR PLANT TO LIFE AND THAT IS IT.

Now, it's your turn

BREWING STAND

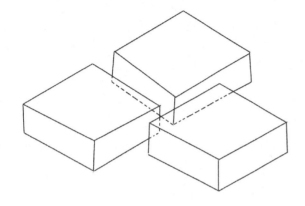

1 FIRST, DRAW THREE SEPARATE CUBES ADJACENT TO ONE ANOTHER, AND THIS IS GOING TO BE THE BASE OF OUR BREWING STAND. ERASE DOTTED LINES.

2 DRAW A VERTICAL RECTANGULAR PRISM AT THE MIDDLE OF THE BASE OF THE BREWING STAND.

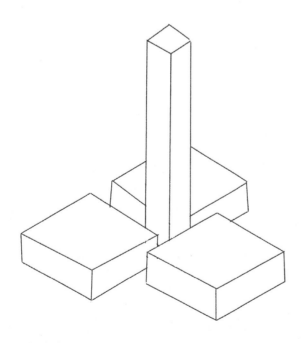

3 THIS IS WHAT IT SHOULD LOOK LIKE WHEN YOU ERASE ALL DOTTED LINES IN STEP 2.

Now, it's your turn

BREWING STAND

4 FOLLOW THISDRAWING TO FORM THE SIDES OF THE BREWING STAND.

5 USE THICKER LINES TO OUTLINE THE FINAL SHAPE OF THE BREWING STAND.

6 ADD SOME FINISHING DETAILS AND IT IS DONE!

Now, it's your turn

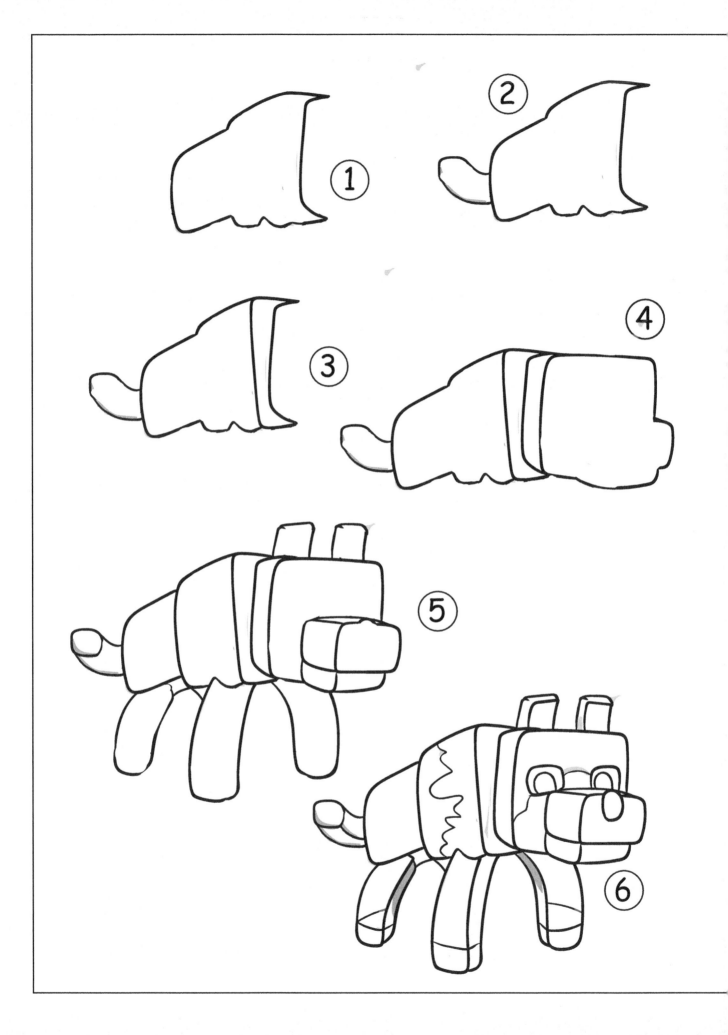

Now, it's your turn

SKELETON

DIFFICULTY LEVEL

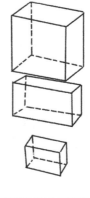

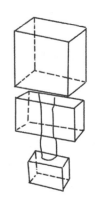

1 FIRST DRAW CUBIC SHAPES FOR HIS HEAD AND BODY

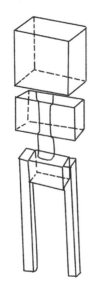

2 DRAW HIS LEGS.

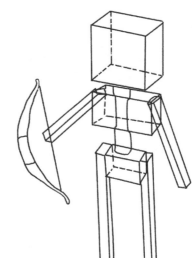

3 NEXT STEP IS TO ADD HIS HANDS AND A BOW ERASE DOTTED LINES

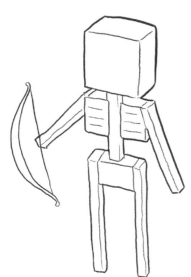

4 ALMOST DONE! NOW WHEN YOU HAVE A SHAPE OF SKELETON'S BODY USE THICKER LINES TO DRAW HIS FINAL SHAPE.

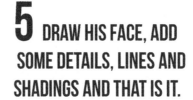

5 DRAW HIS FACE, ADD SOME DETAILS, LINES AND SHADINGS AND THAT IS IT.

Now, it's your turn

Now, it's your turn

ENDERMITE

1 TO DRAW AN ENDERMITE, START WITH A CUBOID, AND DRAW ANOTHER BIGGER ONE BEHIND IT. NEXT DRAW TWO MORE CUBOIDS WITH THE THIRD CUBOID BEING THE LARGEST OF THE FOUR CUBOIDS JUST LIKE IN DRAWING 1A.

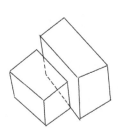

1A

2 CONTINUE STACKING MORE CUBOIDS IN DESCENDING SIZES TO GET THE FINAL SHAPE OF THE ENDERMITES.

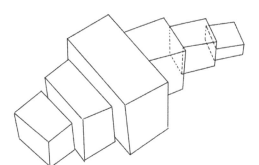

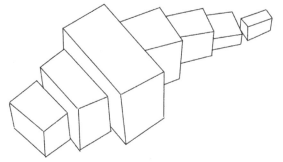

3 FINALLY, USE THICKER LINES TO OUTLINE THE FINAL SHAPE OF THE ENDERMITES, ADD ITS EYES AND SOME SHADINGS.

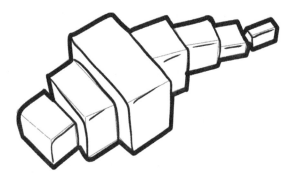

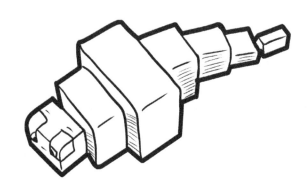

Now, it's your turn

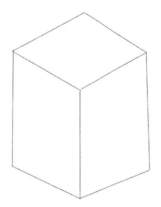

1 START WITH THIS SHAPE FOR HIS HEAD.

2 DRAW HIM A NOSE.

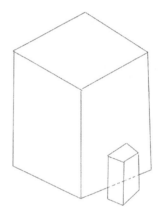

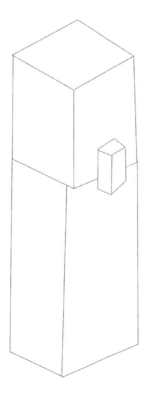

3 DRAW A RECTANGULAR PRISM BELOW HIS HEAD.

Now, it's your turn

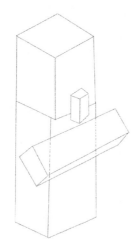

4 DRAW A HORIZONTAL RECTANGULAR PRISM ACROSS THE UPPER PART OF HIS TORSO.

5 NEXT, DRAW HIS SHOULDER AS SHOWN IN THIS STEP.

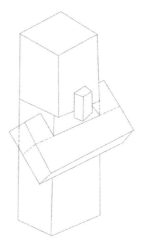

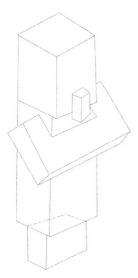

6 ADD A SMALLER CUBOID BELOW HIS BODY TO MAKE HIS FEET AND REMOVE ALL LINE GUIDES.

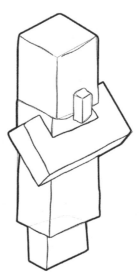

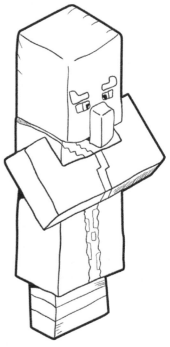

7 NOW YOU CAN TRACE WITH THICKER LINES HIS FINAL SHAPE. DRAW HIS FACE AND DETAILS ON HIS CLOTHING.

Now, it's your turn

VILLAGER

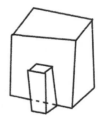

DIFFICULTY LEVEL

1 FIRST DRAW THE SHAPE OF A VILLAGER'S HEAD.

2 ADD HIS ARMS.

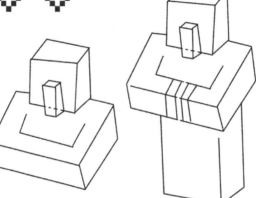

3 NEXT STEP IS EASY. JUST FOLLOW OUR LEAD AND DRAW HIS TORSO

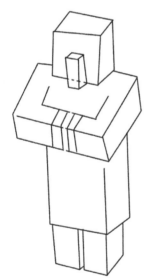

4 NOW JUST ADD HIS LEGS

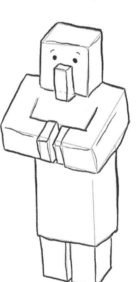

5 ALMOST DONE. NOW DRAW HIS FACE FEATURES

6 FEW MORE DETAILS AND SOME SHADING AND OUR VILLAGER IS DONE.

Now, it's your turn

CHEST

DIFFICULTY LEVEL

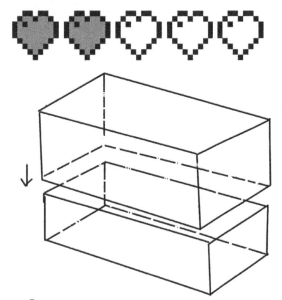

1 DRAW TWO CUBOID AS SHOWN

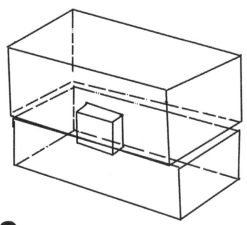

2 NOW DRAW A SMALL CUBOID FOR KEY HOLE. ERASE DOTTED LINES.

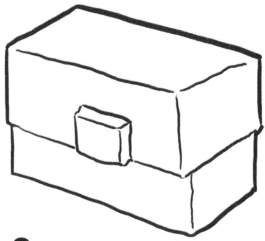

3 ALMOST DONE, NOW WE HAVE SHAPE OF CHEST

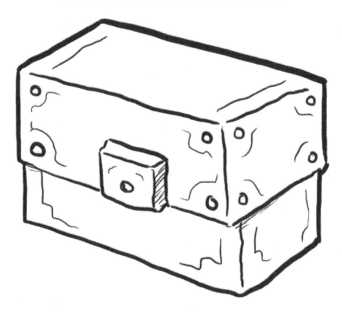

4 TO FINISH ADD SOME DETAILS AND SOME SHADING AND THAT IS IT.

Now, it's your turn

HORSE

1 START WITH THIS BIG CUBOID TO FORM ITS TORSO. AFTER THAT DRAW THE SECOND SHAPE AS SHOWN IN THE SECOND ILLUSTRATION. PAY ATTENTION TO THE MARKED BROKEN LINES, YOU WILL NEED THEM IN THE NEXT STEP.

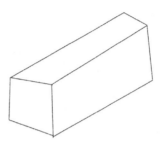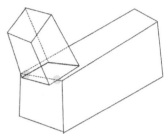

2 USE THE LINES FROM THE UPPER SHAPE AND EXTEND THEM A BIT LIKE WE MARKED IT. DRAW PARALLEL LINES FROM THE MARKED CORNERS, AND STOP WHEN YOU REACHED YOUR EXTENDED LINE. THE SECOND DRAWING SHOWS THE SHAPE OF THE HORSE WE ARE AIMING FOR. ADD THE EARS OF THE HORSE AFTER YOU FINISH DRAWING THE SHAPE OF ITS BODY.

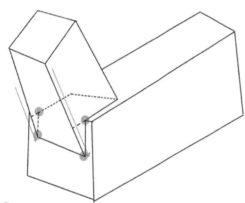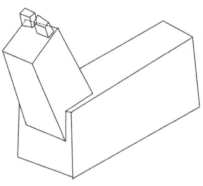

3 ADD ITS SNOUT FOLLOWING THE SHAPE SHOWN IN THE IMAGE BELOW.

4 DRAW ITS LEGS NEXT.

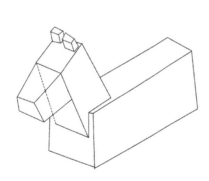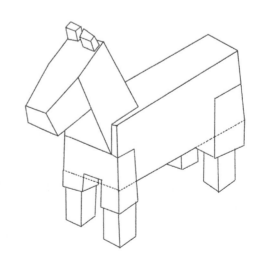

Now, it's your turn

HORSE

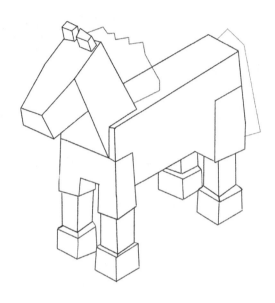

5 ADD FOUR CUBES BELOW ITS LEGS TO CREATE ITS HOOFS. DRAW ITS TAIL AS WELL.

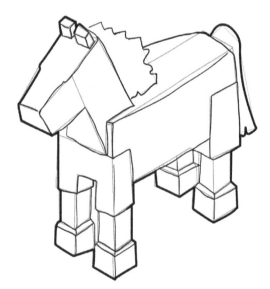

6 TRACE THE OUTLINE OF THE HORSE WITH THICKER LINES TO FORM THE FINAL SHAPE OF THE HORSE

7 NOW FINISH DRAWING YOUR HORSE BY ADDING ITS EYES AND DRAWING ITS THICK MANE.

Now, it's your turn

FURNACE

DIFFICULTY LEVEL

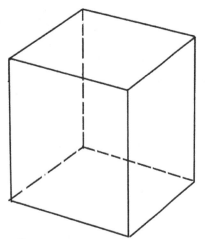

1 DRAW A CUBE LIKE THIS.

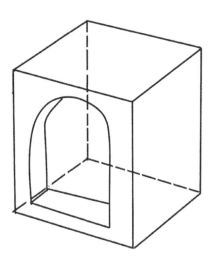

2 NOW DRAW SHAPE LIKE THIS ONE FOR FIRE HOLE, ERASE DOTTED LINES.

3 ALMOST DONE, NOW ADD SOME FLAMES INSIDE OUR SHAPE.

4 ADD SOME SHAPES FOR STONES, AND SOME MORE DETAILS LIKE THIS AND YOU ARE DONE.

Now, it's your turn

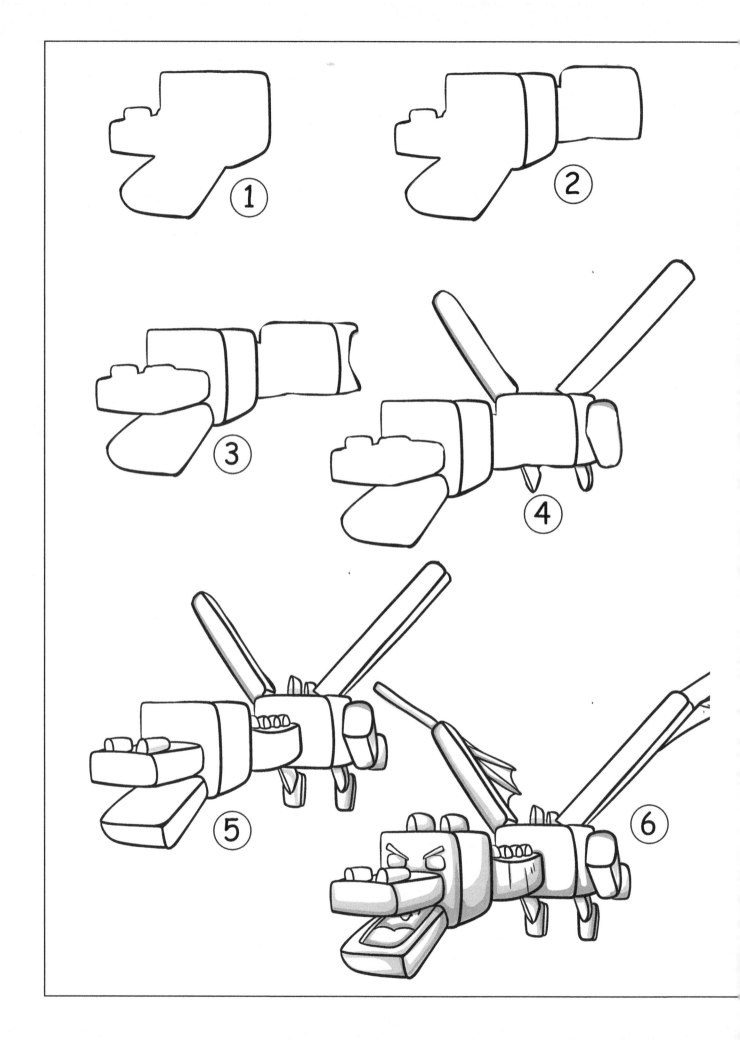

Now, it's your turn

INFINITE FIRE

1 START WITH THIS SHAPE:

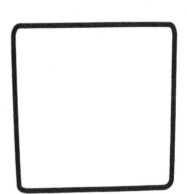

2 NOW, DRAW A FLAME AND A SIDE OF THE BOWL WHICH HOLDS AN INFINITE FIRE.

3 DRAW THE FLAME AND THE SIDE OF THE BOWL WHICH HOLDS THE FIRE.

Now, it's your turn

Now, it's your turn

GHAST

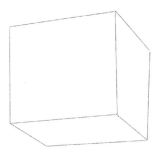

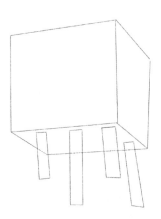

1 TO DRAW A GHAST, FOLLOW THESE STEPS. FIRST, DRAW A CUBE, AFTER THAT DRAW SMALL RECTANGLES FOR ITS LEGS.

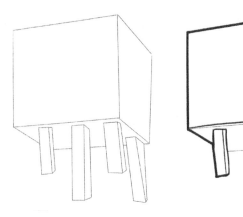

2 MAKE HIS LEGS REALISTIC BY DRAWING ITS SIDES JUST LIKE IN THE LEFT PICTURE.

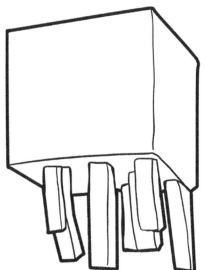

3 LET'S DRAW THIS GHAST EVEN MORE LEGS AND USE THICKER LINES TO TRACE THE FINAL SHAPE OF THE GHAST AND ITS LEGS.

4 TO FINISH IT, JUST DRAW IT A FACE AND SOME LINES FOR SHADING. COOL, ISN'T IT?

Now, it's your turn

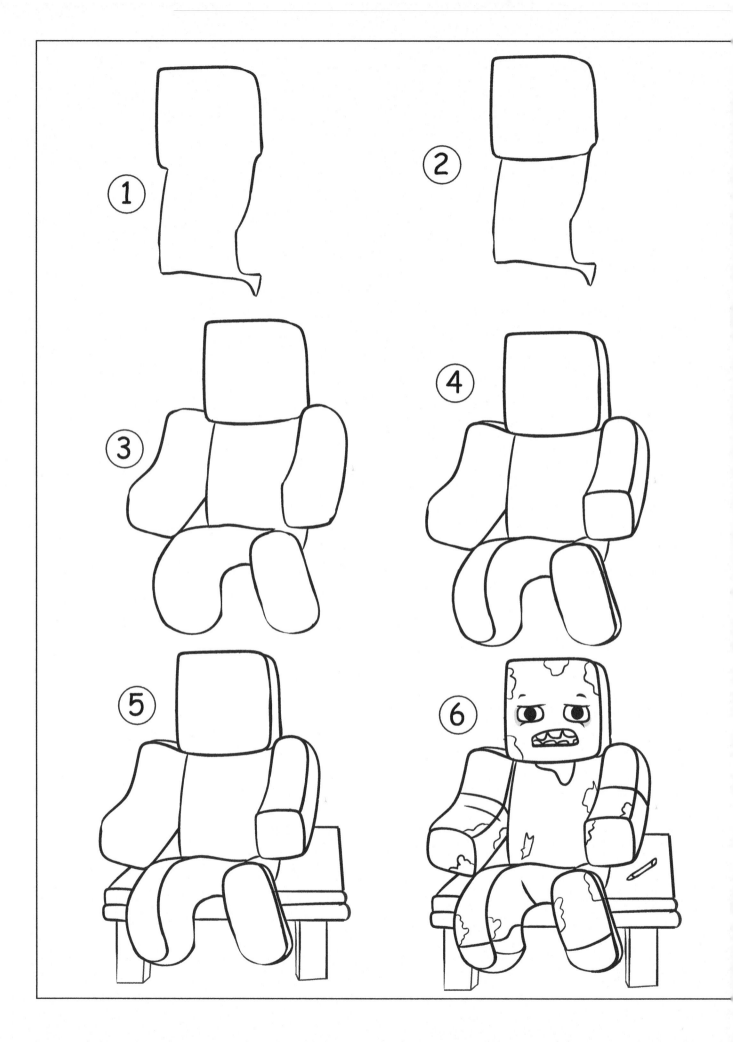

Now, it's your turn

1 START WITH THIS SHAPE:

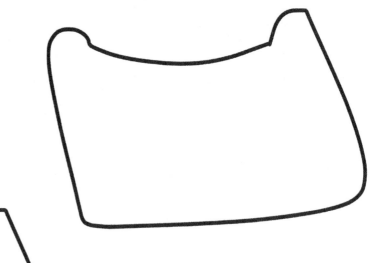

2 DRAW A SHAPE OF A ROLLED PAPER ON EACH SIDE.

3 ALMOST DONE! NOW YOU CAN FINISH YOUR MAP WITH SOME SMALL DETAILS ON THE SIDES, AND OF COURSE, DRAW ANY KIND OF SECRET TREASURE MAP!

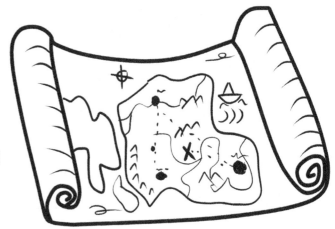

Now, it's your turn

Now, it's your turn

MAGMA CUBE

DIFFICULTY LEVEL

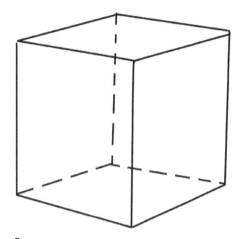

1 DRAW A CUBE.

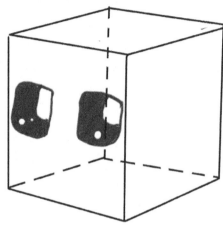

2 NOW DRAW ITS EYES LIKE THIS.

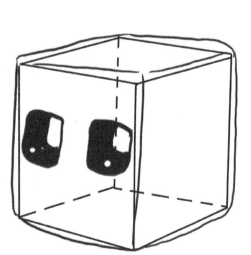

3 MAKE EDGES SOFTER LIKE THIS AND ERASE DOTTED LINES.

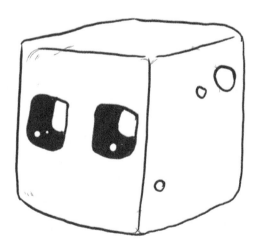

4 ALMOST DONE, JUST ADD SOME ROUND SHAPES FOR DETAILS AND YOU ARE DONE.

Now, it's your turn

Now, it's your turn

Now, it's your turn

CARROT

1 START BY DRAWING THE SHAPE OF THE CARROT.

2 ADD ITS LEAVES.

3 TO FINISH IT, USE THINNER LINES TO DRAW WRINKLES ON ITS BODY AND SOME LINES TO SEPARATE ITS LEAVES.

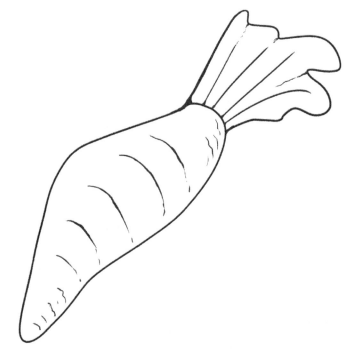

Now, it's your turn

Now, it's your turn

PARROT

1 TO DRAW A PARROT'S HEAD, FOLLOW THE ILLUSTRATIONS SHOWN BELOW. ERASE DOTTED LINES FOR THE NEXT STEP.
2.

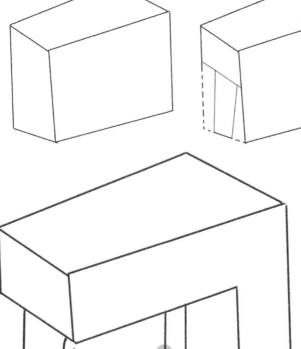

2 LET'S DRAW ITS BEAK! FIRST, FORM A SMALL TRAPEZOID FOLLOWING STEP 1. THAN DRAW A LINE FROM THE MARKED POINT. AND FOR THE LAST STEP DRAW THE LOWER PART OF THE BEAK.

3 NOW YOU CAN FINISH THE SHAPE OF ITS HEAD BY ADDING TALONS ON TOP OF IT.

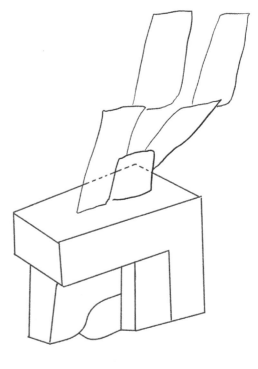

Now, it's your turn

PARROT

4 LET'S DRAW THE REST OF THE BODY! START WITH A LARGE CUBOID FOR ITS BODY AND DRAW A RECTANGLE FOR ITS WINGS. DRAW THE LINE GUIDES FOR ITS FEET AS WELL.

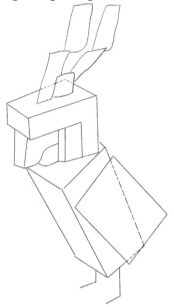

5 ALMOST DONE! DRAW ITS LEG AND FEET. NOW, TRACE WITH THICKER LINES THE FINAL SHAPE OF THE PARROT.

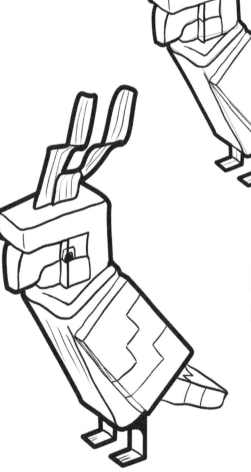

6 TO FINISH DRAWING THE PARROT, DRAW HIS EYE AND TAIL.

Now, it's your turn

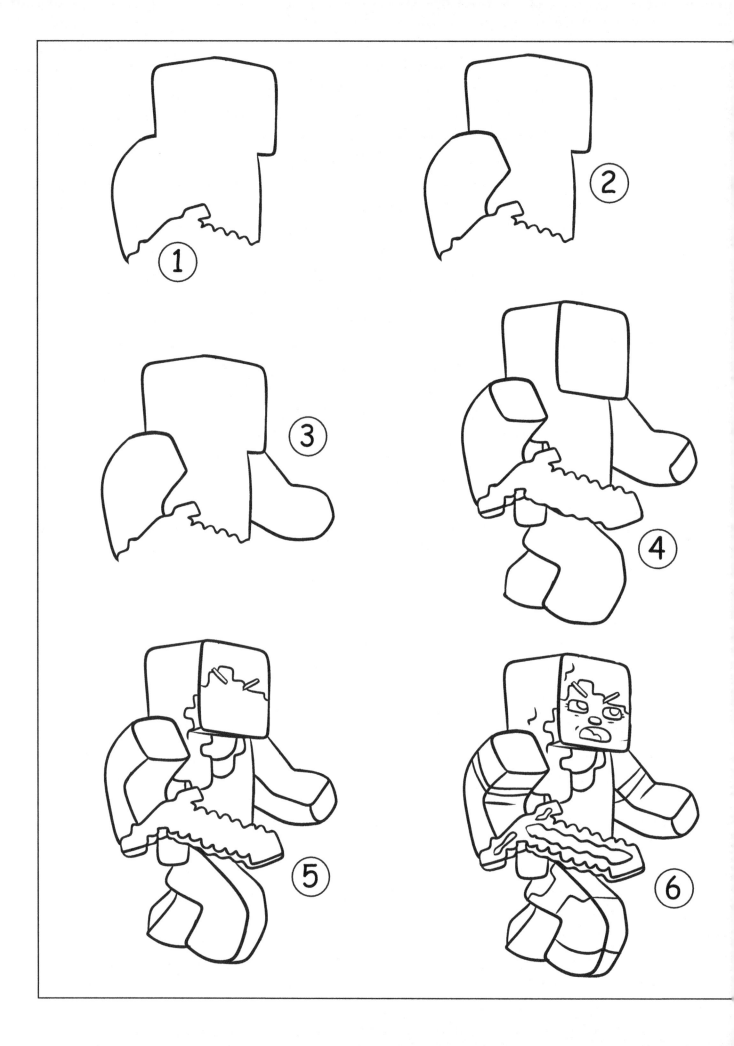

Now, it's your turn

Now, it's your turn

Now, it's your turn

 PIG

1 START FROM THIS SHAPE TO DRAW PIG'S HEAD.

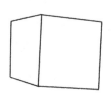 

2 IN THIS STEP, DRAW ITS TORSO

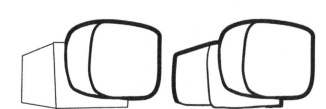

3 NOW, LEGS. START WITH 3 SEPARATE RECTANGLES, CONNECT THEM AND DRAW ONE MORE LIKE IN OUR DRAWING.

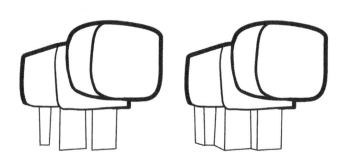

4 TO FINISH YOUR LITTLE PIG, DRAW IT A CUTE FACE, EAR AND A TINY TAIL. YOUR PIG IS CUTE AND DONE!

Now, it's your turn

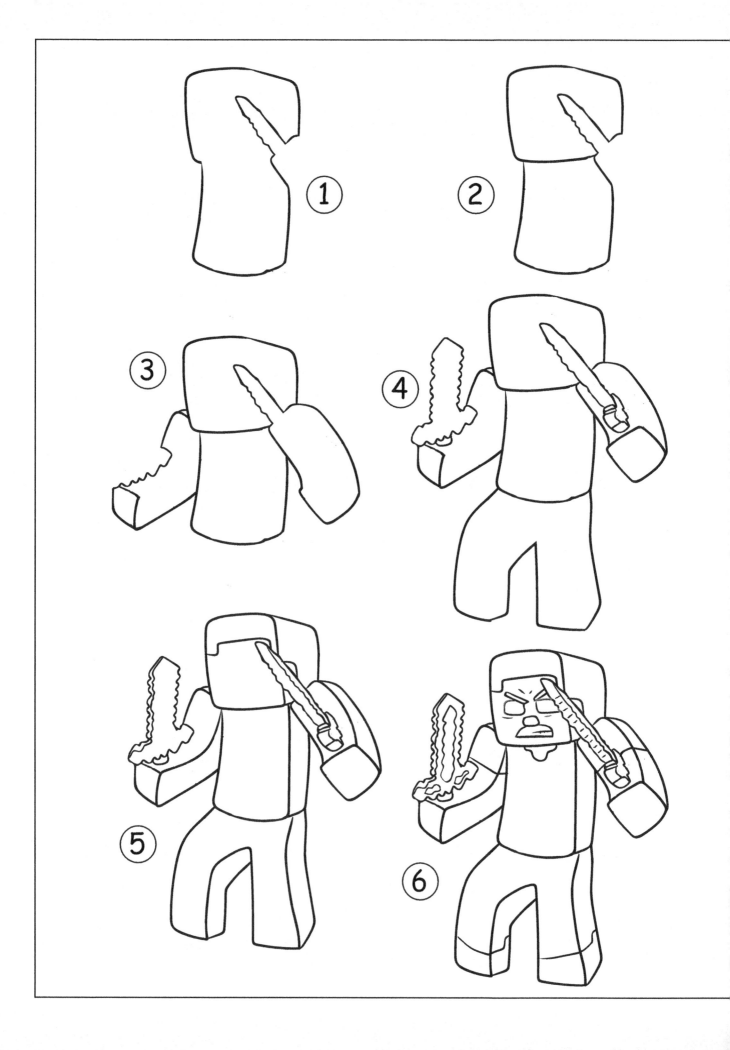

Now, it's your turn

POLAR BEAR

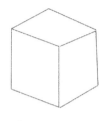
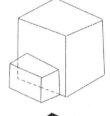
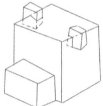

1 START WITH A CUBE TO FORM THE POLAR BEAR'S HEAD. ADD A SMALL RECTANGULAR PRISM TO FORM ITS MOUTH AND FINALLY DRAW TWO SMALLER CUBES TO FORM ITS EARS. TRACE THE HEAD WITH THICKER LINES.

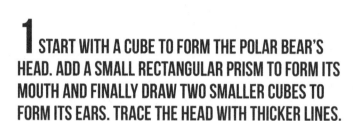

2 TO DRAW THE TORSO, ADD A BIG CUBOID BEHIND THE BEAR'S HEAD JUST LIKE WHAT IS SHOWN IN THE DRAWING.

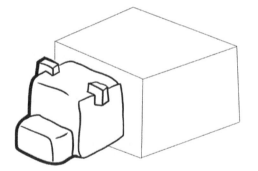

3 NOW UNTO THE SECOND PART OF THE TORSO, DRAW A BIGGER SHAPED CUBE BEHIND THE FIRST PART OF THE TORSO.USING ONE OF THE EDGES AS BASELINE.

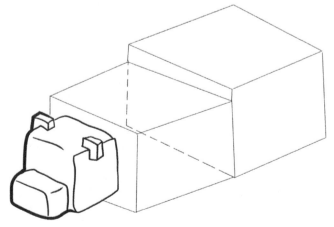

4 SHAPE HIS LEGS USING OUR DRAWINGS BELOW:

5 NOW WHEN YOU HAVE YOUR FINAL GUIDE, USE THICKER LINES TO DRAW THIS POLAR BEAR FULL BODY.

6 TO FINISH THIS BEAR, DRAW IT A FACE AND CLAWS. SHADING AND SOME DETAILS ON ITS FUR WILL MAKE IT NICE AND PRETTY.

Now, it's your turn

Now, it's your turn

SUNFLOWER

DIFFICULTY LEVEL

1 DRAW STEM AND SHAPE OF OUR SUNFLOWER.

2 NOW DRAW ITS LEAVES ON STEM.

3 ALMOST DONE NOW ADD SOME SMALLER PETALS IN THE CENTER OF FLOWER.

4 ADD FEW MORE DETAILS AND OUR SUNFLOWER IS DONE.

Now, it's your turn

PUFFER FISH

1 START WITH A SQUARE WITH A CIRCLE ON ITS EDGE, AFTER THAT, ADD ONE SMALLER SQUARE ON THE UPPER CROSSING, AND ONE MORE ON THE EDGE OF CIRCLE LINE INSIDE THE SQUARE. DRAW THE SHAPE SHOWN IN THE THIRD DRAWING.

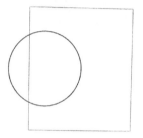 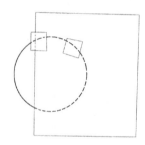 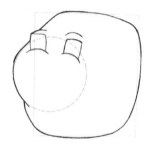

2 ERASE GUIDELINES AND DRAW YOUR FISH FINS AND TAIL.. USE THICKER LINES TO DRAW FINAL SHAPE OF THIS CUTE FISH.

 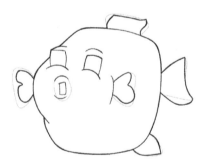

3 TO FINISH PUFFER FISH ADD HER A LOT OF SPIKES. DRAW HER A FACE AND SMALL DETAILS, AND IT IS DONE!

Now, it's your turn

Now, it's your turn

RUBBER SAPLING

DIFFICULTY LEVEL

1 START WITH THE SHAPE OF THE SAPLING.
FIRST DRAW THE MAIN TRUNK AND DRAW FEW BRANCHES ON IT.

2 ADD LEAVES ON ITS BRANCHES.

3 ADD A FEW MORE DETAILS ON ITS TRUNK,
BRANCHES AND LEAVES AND YOUR RUBBER SAPLING
IS FINISHED.

Now, it's your turn

Now, it's your turn

SHULKER

1 1. START WITH SHAPING HIS UPPER PART AND FOLLOWING THESE STEPS.

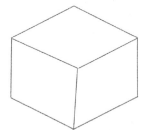
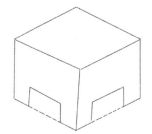
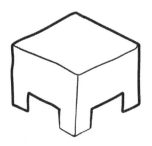

2 NOW FOR THE LOWER PART, FOLLOW THE ILLUSTRATIONS BELOW. IT IS NOT THAT HARD.

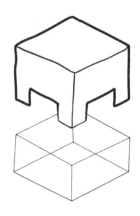
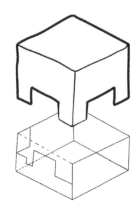
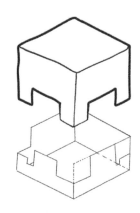
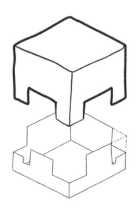

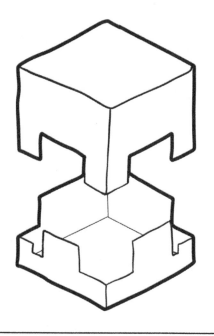

3 USE THICKER LINES TO FORM THE FINAL SHAPE OF HIS SHELL. THIS IS HOW IT SHOULD LOOK LIKE.

Now, it's your turn

SHULKER

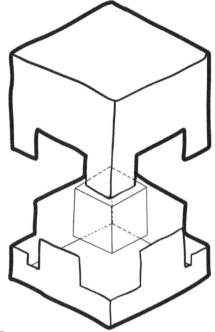

4 NOW FORM HIS MIDDLE PART. REFER TO THE IMAGE TO THE LEFT TO SEE HOW IT IS DONE.

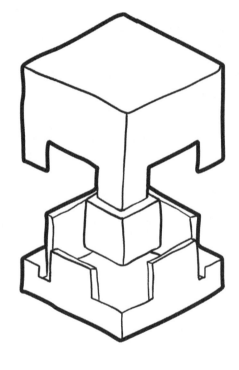

5 ALMOST DONE! USE THICKER LINES TO TRACE THE FINAL SHAPE OF THE SHULKER.

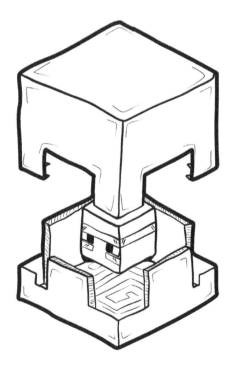

6 NOW WHEN WE HAVE HIS FINAL SHAPE, DRAW HIS FACE AND ADD SMALL DETAILS ON HIS SHELL.

Now, it's your turn

Now, it's your turn

SPRUCE SAPLING

1 OH, THIS ONE IS REALLY EASY. MAKE A SHAPE OF A TRUNK. IT SHOULD BE LONG AND POINTY.

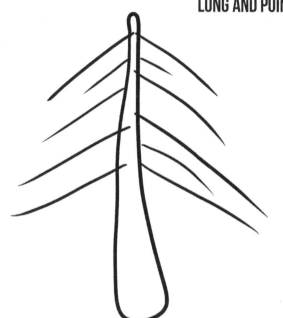

2 NOW, LET'S DRAW SOME LITTLE TWIGS ON IT. JUST DRAW FEW LINES STARTING FROM THE TRUNK.

3 LET'S FINISH IT! DRAW AS MANY LEAVES YOU CAN ON EACH TWIG. TO FINISH IT, ADD SOME SMALL DETAILS ON THE TRUNK AND ON ITS ROOTS.

Now, it's your turn

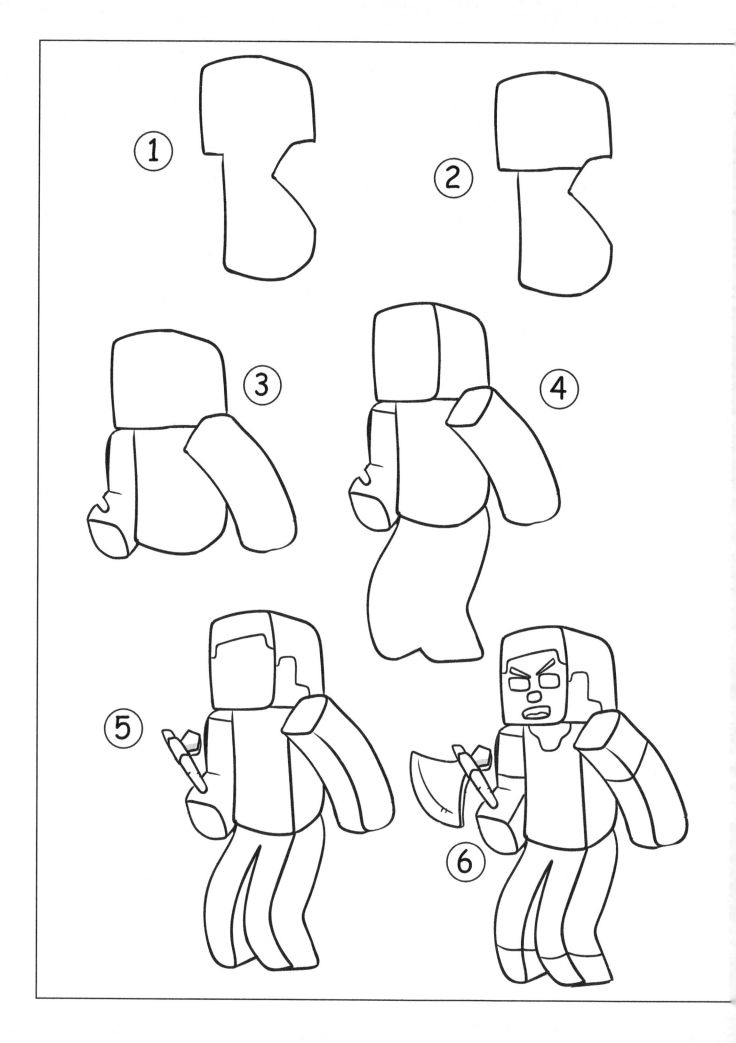

Now, it's your turn

Now, it's your turn

PICKAXE

DIFFICULTY LEVEL

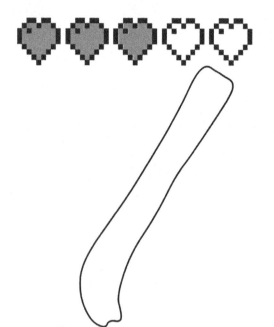

1 DRAW HANDLE SHAPE

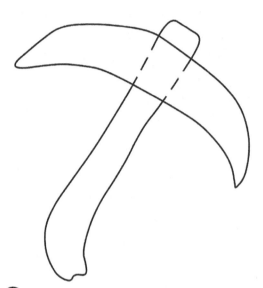

2 NEXT DRAW THIS SHAPE FOR TOP PART OF OUR PICKAXE

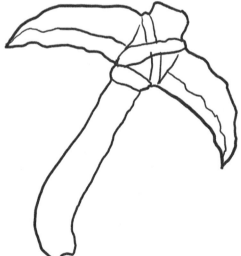

3 ALMOST DONE, ADD SOME LINES FOR ROPE

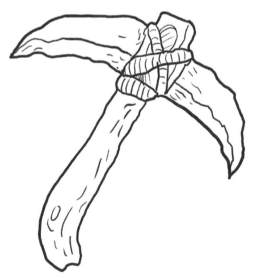

4 ADD SOME MORE LINES AND DETAILS ON THE HANDLE PART FOR WOOD TEXTURE AND WE ARE DONE.

Now, it's your turn

ARMOR STAND

DIFFICULTY LEVEL

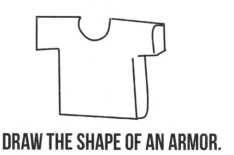

1 DRAW THE SHAPE OF AN ARMOR.

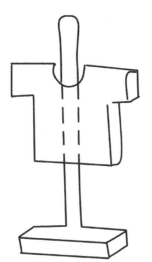

2 DRAW A STAND FOLLOWING THE IMAGE ABOVE.

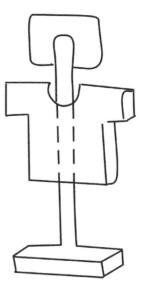

3 NOW DRAW A HELMET.

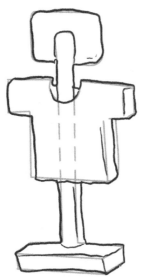

4 FOLLOW LINE GUIDES AND TRACE THE FINAL SHAPE. ERASE ALL LINE GUIDES.

5 TO MAKE IT MORE REALISTIC, USE THIN LINES FOR SMALL DETAILS AND SHADING.

Now, it's your turn

Now, it's your turn

Now, it's your turn

BOAT

DIFFICULTY LEVEL

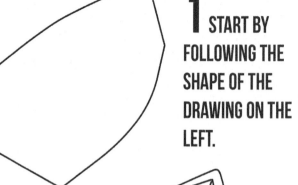

1 START BY FOLLOWING THE SHAPE OF THE DRAWING ON THE LEFT.

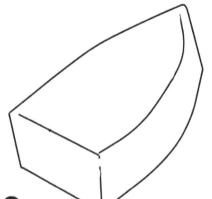

2 FOLLOW OUR DRAWING AND DRAW A SHAPE OF A BOAT.

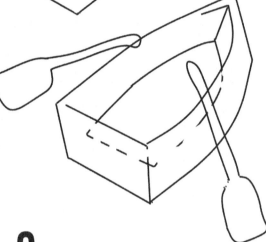

3 NOW, DRAW THE BOTTOM PART OF THE BOAT AND 2 PADDLES.

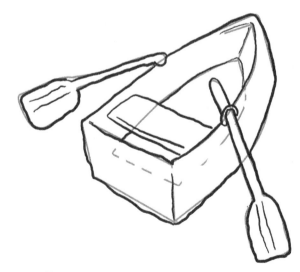

4 FOLLOW THE LINE GUIDES AND TRACE THE FINAL SHAPE OF THE BOAT AND DRAW THE BOAT'S SITTING BENCH.

5 USE SHADINGS AND THIN LINES TO FINISH YOUR DRAWING.

Now, it's your turn

COMPASS

DIFFICULTY LEVEL

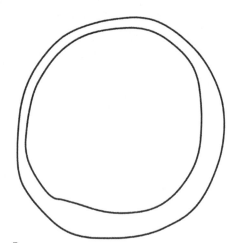

1 DRAW TWO CIRCLES, ONE INSIDE ANOTHER.

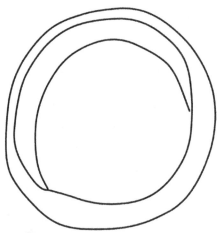

2 FORM A MOON-LIKE SHAPE INSIDE FIRST CIRCLE.

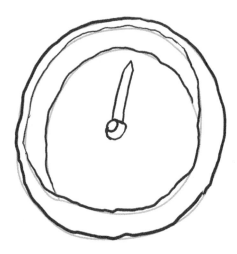

3 USE LINE GUIDES TO TRACE THE SHAPE OF THE COMPASS. DRAW THE NEEDLE OF THE COMPASS.

4 TO FINISH IT, DRAW SOME DETAILS AND ADD GLASS REFLECTION ON THE COMPASS.

Now, it's your turn

SHEARS

DIFFICULTY LEVEL

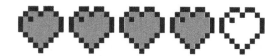

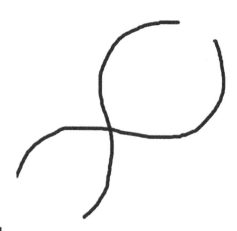

1 DRAW TWO WAVY LINES CROSSING EACH OTHER LIKE THE DRAWING ABOVE.

2 USE THE LINE GUIDES TO DRAW THE SHAPE OF THE SHEARS.

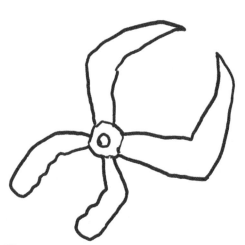

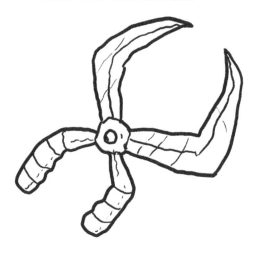

3 DRAW A JOINING SCREW AT THE CENTER OF THE SHEARS AND ERASE LINE GUIDES.

4 TO FINISH IT, ADD SOME DETAILS ON HANDLES AND BLADES.

Now, it's your turn

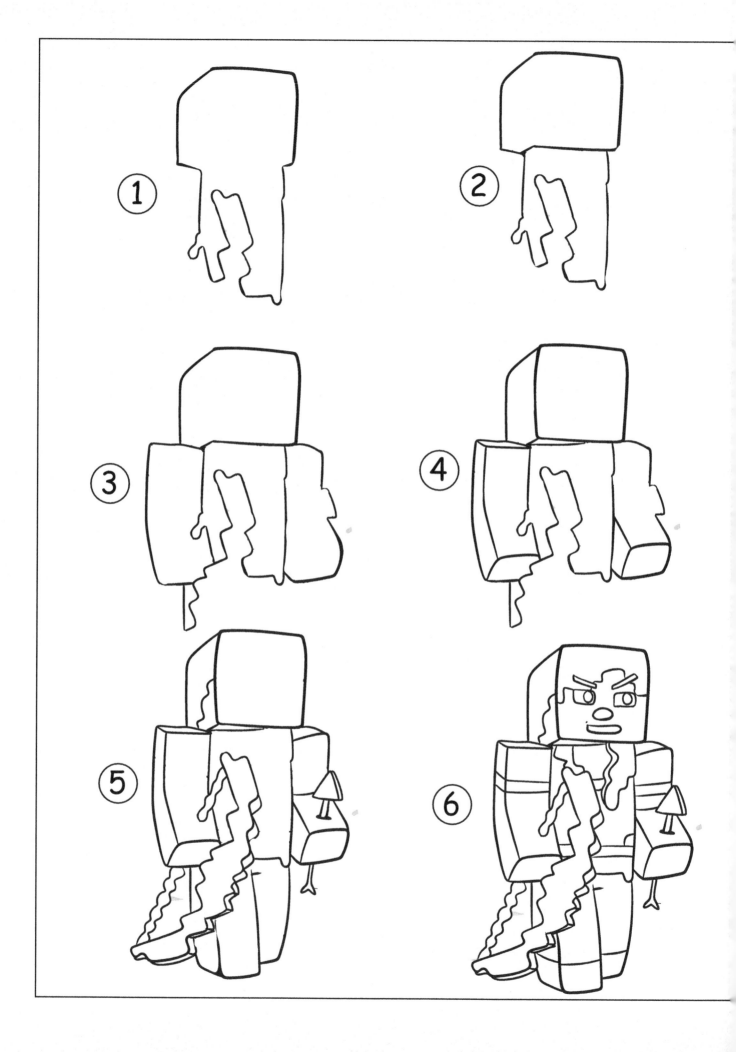

Now, it's your turn

STEVE

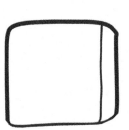

1 START WITH THE SHAPE OF HIS HEAD.

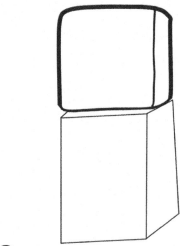

2 THEN DRAW HIS TORSO.

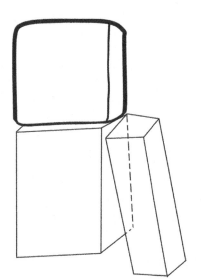

3 NOW LET'S SHAPE HIS LEFT ARM.
FOLLOW THE DRAWING AND ERASE DOTTED LINES.

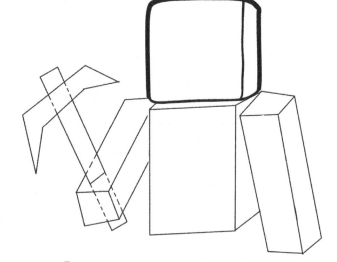

4 LET'S DRAW HIS OTHER ARM. FIRST DRAW
AN ARM THEN SHAPE A PICKAXE.

Now, it's your turn

STEVE

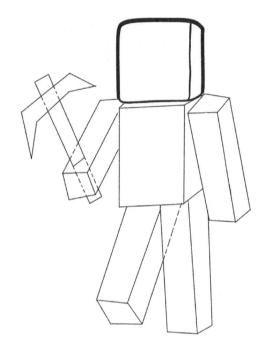

5 NOW THAT WE HAVE THE SHAPE OF HIS UPPER BODY, LET'S DRAW HIS LEGS JUST LIKE IN THE PICTURE.

6 USE THICKER LINES TO OUTLINE THE FINAL SHAPE OF STEVE'S BODY.

7 TO FINISH DRAWING STEVE, DRAW HIS FACE AND HAIR. ADD SOME SHADINGSAND DETAILS ON HIS CLOTHES AND PICKAXE. YOUR STEVE IS DONE.

Now, it's your turn

SWORD

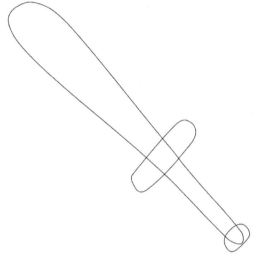

1 SHAPE A SWORD USING THESE THREE SHAPES.

2 NOW, LET'S MAKE IT POINTY! FOLLOW THE DRAWING ABOVE AND FORM A SWORD.

3 ADD LINES ON THE SWORD TO SEPARATE THE HANDLE FROM THE BLADE. ADD DETAILS ON ITS BLADE TO MAKE IT LOOK REALLY SHARP.

4 ALMOST DONE! NOW YOU CAN FINISH YOUR DRAWING WITH SOME SMALL DETAILS ON THE HANDLE.

Now, it's your turn

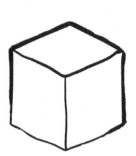

1 OKAY, FIRST STEP IS EASY SO LET'S BEGIN! START WITH A CUBE FOR HIS HEAD.

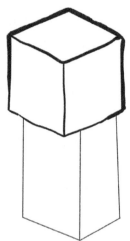

2 NOW, DRAW HIM A TORSO.

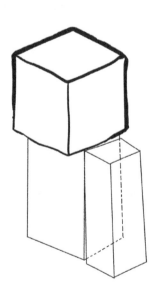

3 NEXT STEP IS HIS LEFT ARM. DRAW SHAPE OF IT NEXT TO THE BODY.

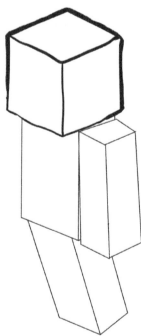

4 WE CAN NOW DRAW HIM HIS LEGS FOLLOWING THE DRAWING ABOVE.

Now, it's your turn

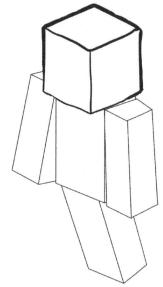

5 NOW DRAW HIM HIS OTHER ARM.

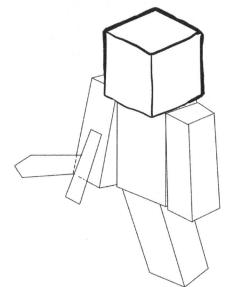

6 LET'S DRAW THE SHAPE OF HIS SWORD IN HIS RIGHT HAND.

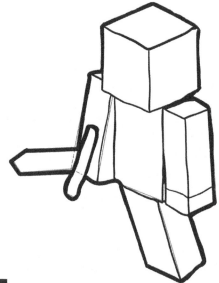

7 USE THICKER LINES TO TRACE THE FINAL SHAPE OF HIS BODY. ERASE ALL GUIDELINES.

8 FINALLY, LET'S DRAW HIS LEFT WING. AFTER THAT, ADD HIS FACE, SOME DETAILS ON HIS SWORD AND HIS BODY.

Now, it's your turn

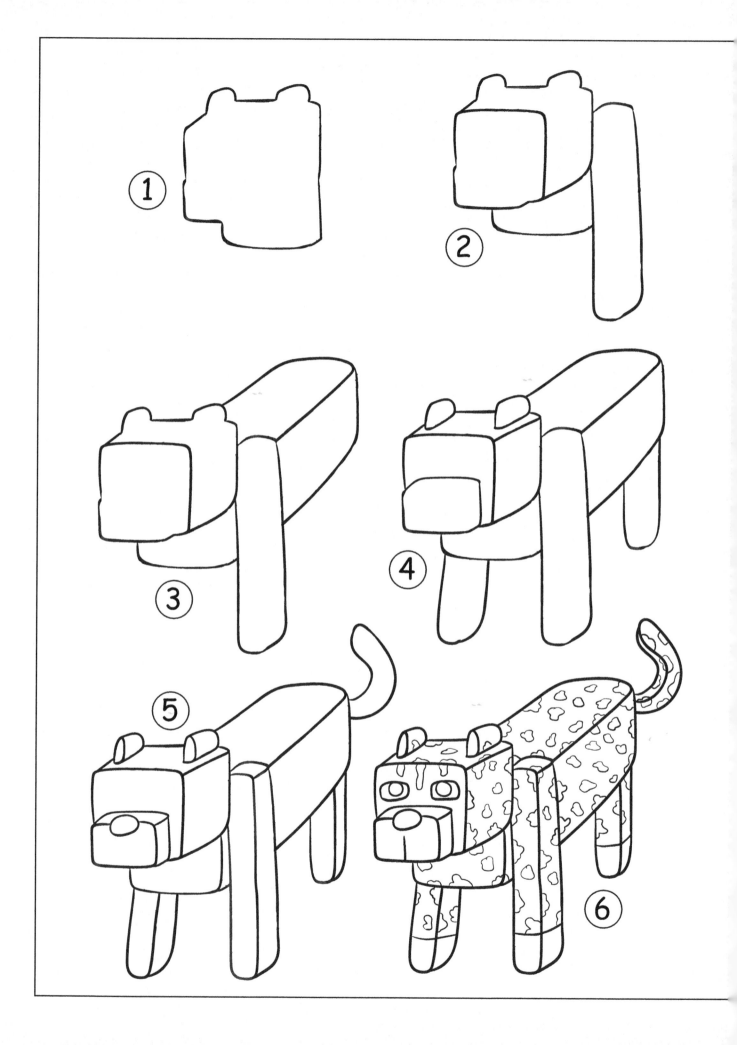

Now, it's your turn

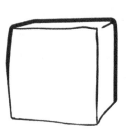

1 TO START, DRAW A CUBE FOR HIS HEAD.

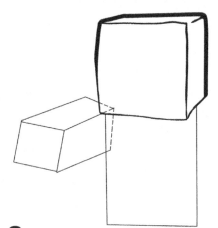

2 DRAW A RECTANGLE FOR HIS TORSO AND SHAPE HIS RIGHT ARM.

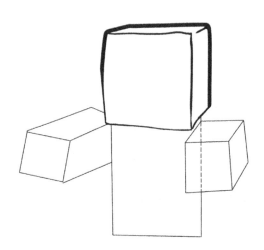

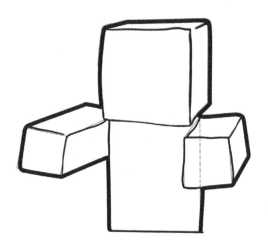

3 NOW, DRAW THE LEFT ARM AND THEN SHAPE HIS UPPER BODY WITH THICKER LINES.

Now, it's your turn

ZOMBIE

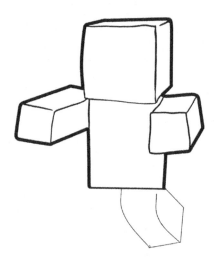

4 DRAW ONE OF HIS LEGS.

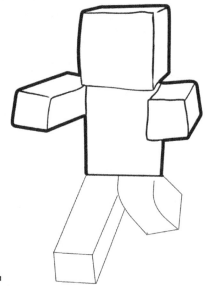

5 NOW YOU CAN SHAPE ANOTHER LEG FOLLOWING OUR DRAWING.

6 NOW WHEN WE HAVE THE SHAPE OF HIS BODY, LET'S FINISH THE DRAWING.

7 TO FINISH DRAWING THE ZOMBIE, MAKE HIS CLOTHES OLD AND DRAW HIS FACE WITH FEW SPOTS ON HIS HEAD.

Now, it's your turn

WHEAT

DIFFICULTY LEVEL

1 START WITH THIS FUNNY SHAPE.

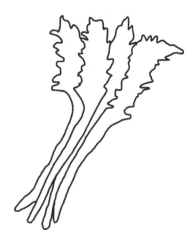

2 NOW, TRY TO COPY FIRST SHAPE AND DRAW SEVERAL OF THEM FORMING A BUSHEL.

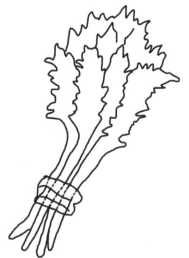

3 DRAW SOME MORE LEAVES ON TOP AND A CORD AROUND TWIGS.

4 TRACE OUR GUIDELINES AND DRAW A FINAL SHAPE OF WHEAT BUSHEL.

5 TO FINISH IT, USE THINNER LINES FOR SOME SMALL DETAILS AND SHADINGS.

Now, it's your turn

VINDICATOR

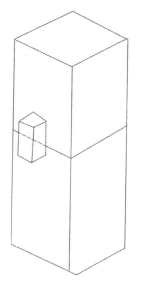

1 START BY DRAWING A VERTICAL RECTANGULAR PRISM. SEPARATE HIS BODY AND HEAD BY ADDING A HORIZONTAL LINE ON THE UPPER PART OF THE PRISM. DRAW HIM HIS NOSE

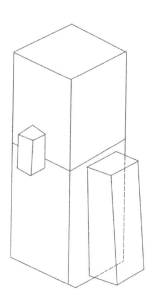

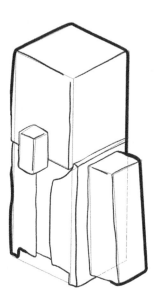

2 DRAW THE SHAPE SHOWN ABOVE WHERE HIS ARM SHOULD BE.

3 FOLLOW THE LINE GUIDES AND DRAW THE FINAL SHAPE OF HIS UPPER BODY IN A SUIT.

Now, it's your turn

VINDICATOR

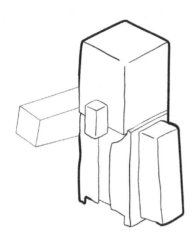

4 NOW, DRAW THE SHAPE OF HIS OTHER ARM.

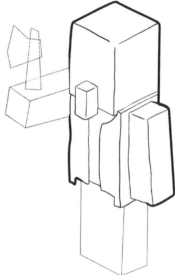

5 NEXT STEP ARE LEGS AND A SHAPE OF AN AXE WHICH HE IS HOLDING.

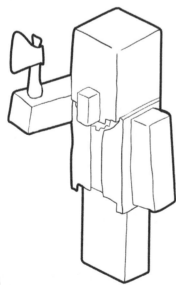

6 USE THICKER LINES TO DRAW THE FINAL SHAPE OF HIS LOWER BODY AND HIS AXE.

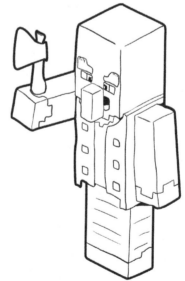

7 TO FINISH THIS DRAWING, DRAW HIS FACE AND ADD DETAILS ON HIS CLOTHES. USE SHADES AND THIN LINES TO MAKE HIM LOOK SCARY.

Now, it's your turn

MINECART

DIFFICULTY LEVEL

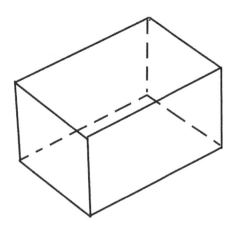

1 START WITH A RECTANGULAR CUBOID SHAPE.

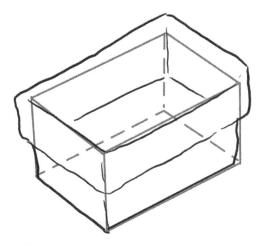

2 FORM THE SHAPE OF THE MINECART USING THE GUIDELINES.

3 ERASE GUIDELINES AND ADD WHEELS ON MINECART.

4 TO FINISH IT, ADD SOME DETAILS ON EDGES AND SHADINGS.

Now, it's your turn

1 LET'S START FROM THE TOP! TO DRAW WITCH HAT YOU SHOULD FOLLOW THESE STEPS:

  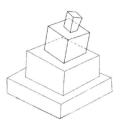 

2 NOW, DRAW A RECTANGULAR PRISM TO FORM HER BODY.

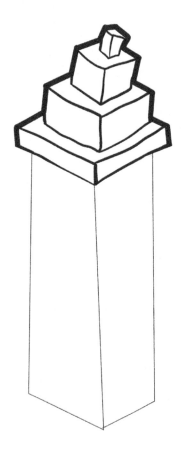

3 SEPARATE HER BODY AND HEAD BY ADDING A HORIZONTAL LINE ON THE UPPER PART OF THE PRISM.

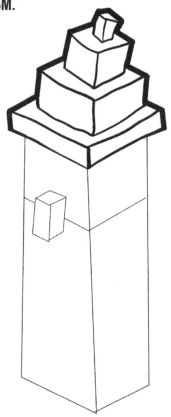

Now, it's your turn

WITCH

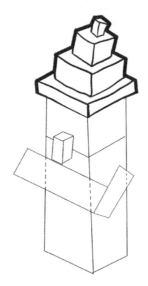

4 TO START FORMING HER HANDS, DRAW A RECTANGLE UNDER HER NOSE. AFTER THAT, DRAW SMALLER ONE, JUST LIKE IN OUR DRAWING.

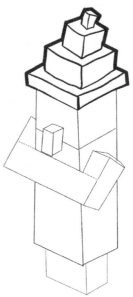

5 TO FINISH WITCH'S HANDS, FOLLOW OUR DRAWING. ADD HER LEGS. ERASE DOTTED LINES - AND WE HAVE A FULL SHAPE OF HER BODY.

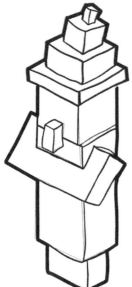

6 NOW, WE HAVE THE SHAPE OF HER BODY. USE THICKER LINES TO DRAW HER FULL SHAPE, JUST LIKE THIS!

7 ALMOST DONE! DRAW HER A FACE, MOLE ON HER NOSE AND SOME DETAILS ON HER HAT AND CLOTHES. NOW SHE IS FINISHED!

Now, it's your turn

PUMPKIN

DIFFICULTY LEVEL

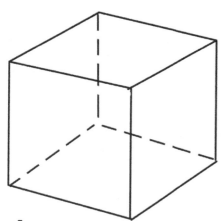

1 FIRST DRAW A CUBE.

2 TRACE THE GUIDELINES AND DRAW
A PUMPKIN SHAPE. ADD ITS EYES AND MOUTH,

3 ALMOST DONE, NOW YOU HAVE
THE SHAPE OF THE PUMPKIN.

4 TO FINISH PUMPKIN, DRAW IT A PEDICEL
AND SOME SHADINGS.

Now, it's your turn

DIFFICULTY LEVEL

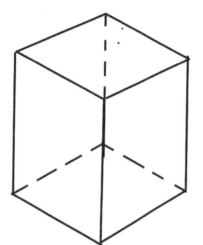

1 START WITH A LARGE CUBE.

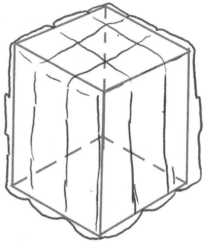

2 FOLLOW THE DRAWINGS ABOVE AND TRACE THE SHAPE OF THE TNT.

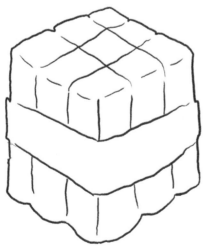

3 ERASE EXCESSIVE LINES AND DRAW THE LABEL FOR THE TNT.

4 WRITE TNT ON THE LABEL AND DRAW A FEW WICKS AND IT'S DONE.

Now, it's your turn

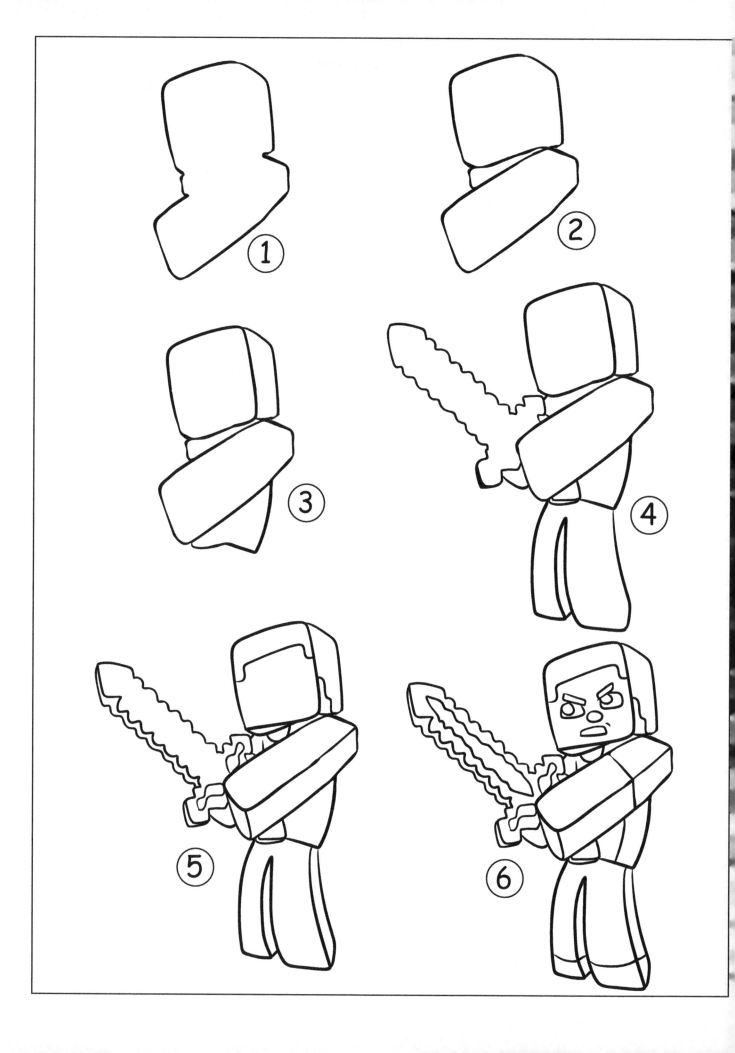

Now, it's your turn

DIFFICULTY LEVEL

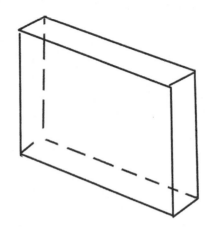

1 DRAW A FLAT RECTANGULAR CUBOID JUST LIKE IN OUR DRAWING.

2 DRAW A SMALL CUBE ON THE UPPER MIDDLE PART OF THE SIGN AND DRAW A LONG VERTICAL RECTANGULAR CUBOID BELOW THE SIGN.

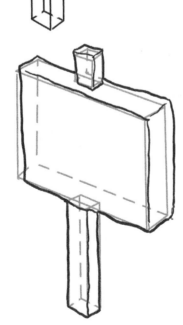

3 TRACE LINES TO DRAW THE FINAL SHAPE OF OUR SIGN.

4 DRAW SMALL DETAILS AND SHADING, AND WE HAVE SIGN!

Now, it's your turn

SPRUCE

DIFFICULTY LEVEL

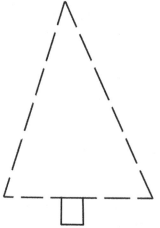

1 FIRST, DRAW A TRIANGLE WITH A SMALL SQUARE BELOW IT.

2 DRAW WAVY HORIZONTAL LINES ALONG THE SIDES OF THE TRIANGLE AND FORM THE SHAPE OF THE SPRUCE.

3 ERASE GUIDELINES AND USE THICKER LINES TO FORM THE SHAPE OF THE SPRUCE.

4 ADD SOME SMALL DETAILS, AND HERE IT IS!

Now, it's your turn

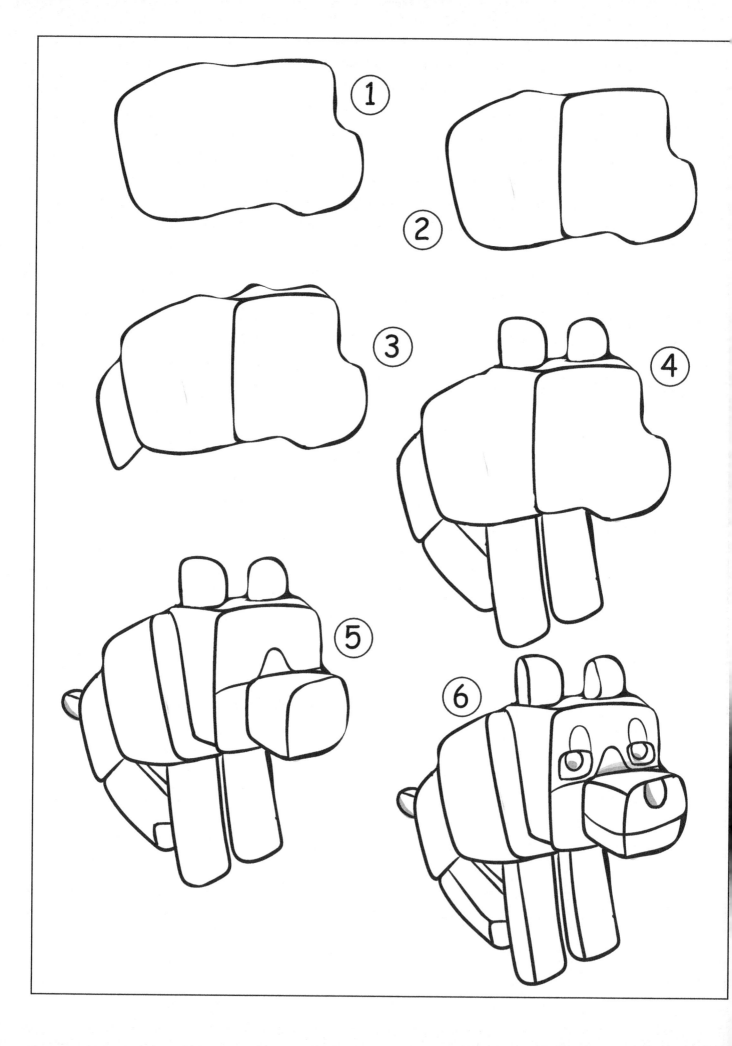

Now, it's your turn

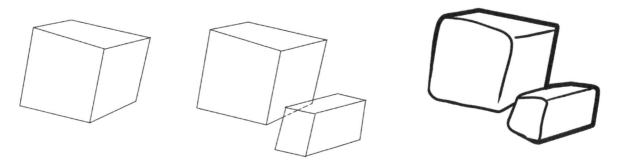

1 FOLLOW THESE THREE SIMPLE STEPS TO FORM THE SHAPE OF HIS HEAD AND LEFT ARM.

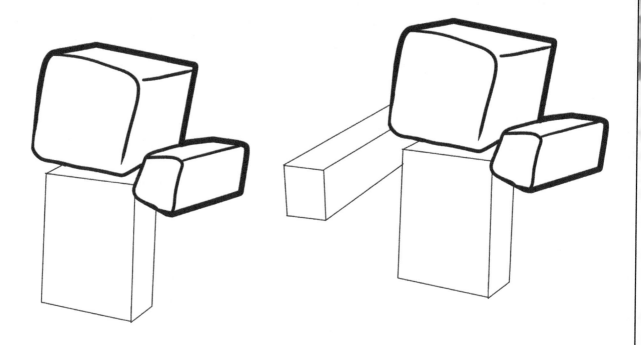

2 DRAW HIM A TORSO FOLLOWING THE IMAGE ABOVE.

3 NOW DRAW HIS RIGHT ARM.

Now, it's your turn

ZOMBIE PIGMAN

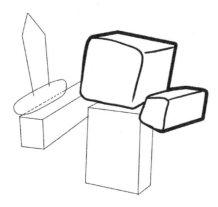

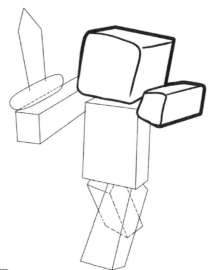

4 DRAW THE SHAPE OF A SWORD ON HIS RIGHT HAND.

5 LET'S PROCEED WITH HIS LEGS. FIRST, FORM THE LEFT LEG, THEN DRAW HIS RIGHT ONE BEHIND LEFT.

6 USE THICKER LINES TO DRAW HIS FINAL BODY SHAPE.

7 NOW, LET'S FINISH THIS DRAWING AND MAKE HIM LOOK CREEPY AND SCARY BY DRAWING HIS FACE AND ADDING DETAILS ON HIS BODY.

Now, it's your turn

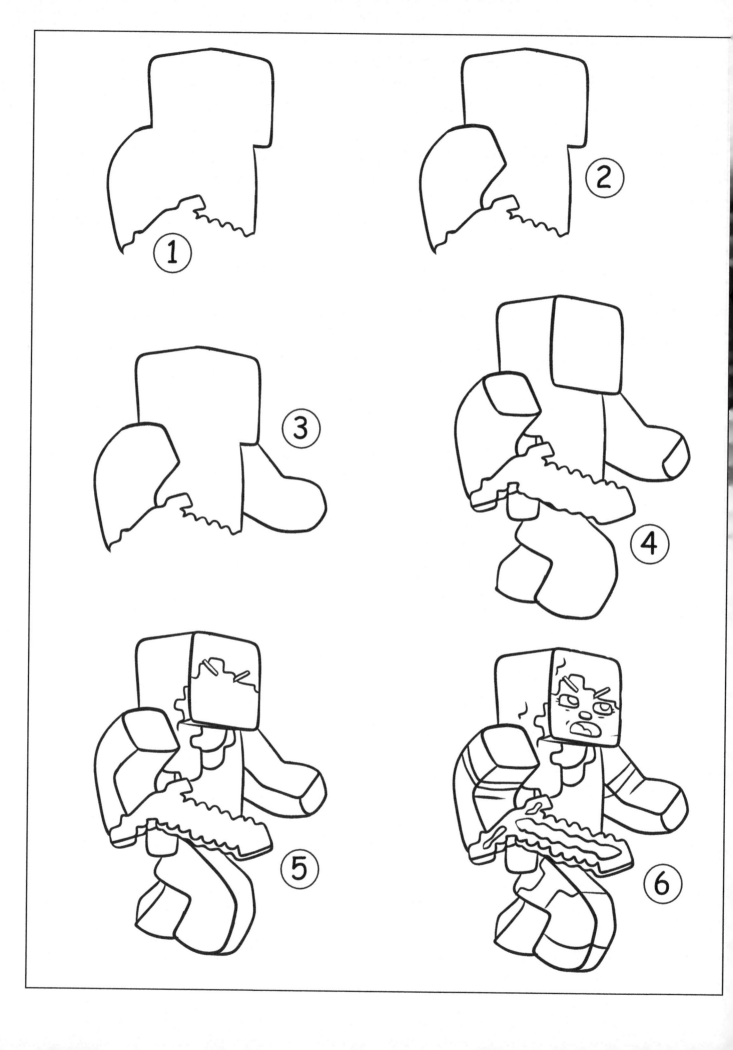

Now, it's your turn

POTION

1 TO DRAW A POTION, START WITH A SHAPE OF A BOTTLE. TRY TO DRAW SOMETHING LIKE THIS:

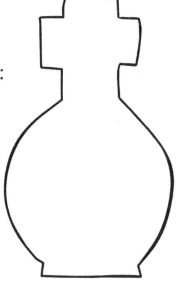

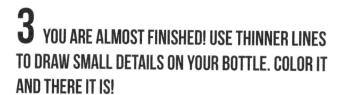

2 SEPARATE THE BOTTLE FROM THE CORK. DRAW A SHADING OF A GLASS REFLECTION ON THE BOTTLE.

3 YOU ARE ALMOST FINISHED! USE THINNER LINES TO DRAW SMALL DETAILS ON YOUR BOTTLE. COLOR IT AND THERE IT IS!

Now, it's your turn

Made in the USA
Coppell, TX
27 June 2021